Earth Wisdom

Hay House Titles of Related Interest

Books

Healing with the Fairies, by Doreen Virtue

The Way of Wyrd, by Brian Bates

Wiccan Healing, by Sally Morningstar (available from March 2005)

Card Decks

Power Animals, by Steven D. Farmer

All of the above are available at your local bookshop or may be ordered by visiting:

Hay House UK: www.hayhouse.co.uk

Hay House USA: www.hayhouse.com

Hay House Australia: www.hayhouse.com.au

Hay House South Africa: orders@psdprom.co.za

Earth Wisdom

A Heartwarming Mixture of the Spiritual, the Practical and the Proactive

Glennie Kindred

All illustrations by Glennie Kindred

HAY HOUSE, INC.

Australia – Canada – Hong Kong

South Africa – United Kingdom – United States

Copyright © 2004 Glennie Kindred

Published and distributed in the United Kingdom by:
Hay House UK, Ltd, Unit 62, Canalot Studios, 222 Kensal Rd, London W10 5BN
Phone: 44-20-8962-1230 • Fax: 44-20-8962-1239 • www.hayhouse.co.uk

Published and distributed in the United States by:
Hay House, Inc., P.O. Box 5100, Carlsbad, CA 92018-5100
Phone: 760-431-7695 or 800-654-5126 • Fax: 760-431-6948 or 800-650-5115 • www.hayhouse.com

Published and distributed in Australia by:
Hay House Australia, Ltd, 18/36 Ralph St., Alexandria NSW 2015
Phone: 61-2-9669-4299 • Fax: 61-2-9669-4144 • www.hayhouse.com.au

Published and distributed in the Republic of South Africa by:
Hay House SA (Pty), Ltd, P.O. Box 990, Witkoppen 2068
Phone/Fax: 27-11-701-2233 • orders@psdprom.co.za

Distributed in Canada by:
Raincoast, 9050 Shaughnessy St., Vancouver, B.C. V6P 6E5
Phone: 604-323-7100 • Fax: 604-323-2600

Design: e-Digital
Edited by Lizzie Hutchins
All artwork © Glennie Kindred

The author reserves her moral rights in this work.

A catalogue record for this book is available from the British Library

07 06 05 04   4 3 2 1
1st printing, August 2004
ISBN 1-4019-0471-8

Printed in Europe by Imago

Dedicated
to all of Earth's children
and to all of the people
whose Love
and generosity of Spirit
are creating
positive change
in the world.

'The point of power is always in the present moment.'
Louise L. Hay

TOWARDS A

Be mindful!
Husband the earth. Protect her from greed and violence. Build humbly, plant trees, grow flowers and clothe her with dignity. Respect all her creatures. Honour her natural laws and the universe which cradles her. Above all, heartily worship the Source of All that Is.

This world needs secret heroes! Be brave, speak the truth, heal the sick, make peace. Be strong, serve patiently, love generously, live simply. Enjoy fellowship, eat and drink modestly, celebrate the festivals. Breathe deeply, sing and make music, walk often, cycle and recycle. Be thrifty, prefer cashflow to possession, give good measure. Let your work be your prayer.

Put on the whole armour of light! Unearth the beauty in everything. Inhale the Spirit of Goodness. Kindle kindness, especially toward yourself, embracing the sweet silence of your own soul. Fear nothing. Accept what you are and—while you have breath—give thanks.

TRUE BALANCE

Exhortation : Towards a True Balance
by John P. Rogers © 1987.
All rights reserved.

See Appendix page 279 for purchase details.

Contents

Preface

I am writing this book with an awareness that our world is changing.

A new global consciousness is emerging and it is disrupting the old 'us and them' mentality that has, until now, supported a world held in conflict, fear and separation.

We are changing.

People all over the world, from different backgrounds, different cultures and different belief systems, are uniting in a new feeling, a sense of a global 'We'.

The 'We' consciousness is emerging out of our evolutionary needs. It is not being imposed upon us but is willingly being embraced, chosen and understood on a level that goes beyond words.

We feel a growing responsibility to help each other and to move closer together as one global family. Our hearts are open, generous and loving. We support life and each and everyone's basic right to happiness. Our compassion is strong and we act on it.

We are willing to serve the common good and protect the environment from further harm. Our expanding communication systems mean that we are no longer isolated or ignorant about what is happening around the world.

We are willing to trust our intuition and have the courage to follow our dreams and visions.

We are standing together, knowing our strength lies in this feeling of togetherness. We are choosing to take the path of the heart, the path of Love and goodwill. We are aware of the power inherent in all our acts of goodness.

Love is at the heart of all the world's spiritual teachings. It is not a new idea, but the power of Love is on the move, gathering momentum, happiness and liberation, and inspiring a change of heart in the world.

This is our voyage of discovery, our delightful rebellion and our profoundly exhilarating act of adaptation. It is a potent evolutionary shift, having as much survival value and significance as any physical transformation.

I plant this book like a seed in the Earth. It is your seed, my seed, a seed of our future. May we grow strong and true.

Glennie Kindred 2004.

Thanks to the commitment of the
team at Hay House UK, this book has
been printed on chlorine-free recycled paper.

It is our wish that more publishers
will follow this lead, so that more trees can continue
to live and energise the Air we all breathe.

With Special Thanks and Gratitude

To my partner, Brian Boothby, for your deep goodness of Spirit, good humour and constant support.

To my children, Jerry, Jack and May, for being honest and true, and making me laugh and cry at the same time.

To my mum, Margaret Newman, for your loving nature and for being open and honest with me.

To Maggie Norman, for being a truly good friend, for your clarity and for sharing the experience with me.

To the Elementals: Jayne Paulson, Jeannie Thompson, Marion McCartney and Rosemary Greenwood, for your open-hearted Love and support and the joy of being together as we share our commitment to positive change.

To Jim Banting and the design team at e-Digital for a joyful and superb production process.

To Lizzie Hutchins for brilliant and sensitive editing.

To Michelle Pilley and all at Hay House UK, for all your encouragement, generosity and hard work on my behalf.

Part
One

All Things
Are
Connected

The first part of this book lays down the foundations for the path of Earth wisdom. It explores some of the Celtic traditions, knowledge and beliefs from Britain and Northern Europe and brings them forward to the present day.

The second part of the book provides practical ideas for making seasonal connections.

Every chapter has its own tree to help us to link to the message and information in the chapter and to the wisdom of the Earth.

All things are connected.

WE
Are the
Change

Our planet Earth is a Wonder.

When we are touched by Nature, we are lifted out of time, beyond our everyday lives, to a place of inner stillness, wonder and Oneness with life. We become part of the invisible unity that holds all life together. The most profound and yet the simplest experiences pass through our brains to touch our hearts. This is a simple truth. The more we allow the beauty of Nature and acts of natural goodness to touch our hearts, the more deeply we celebrate our natural spiritual connection to life.

Earlier civilizations the world over understood the essential unity of life

3

and respected everything on Earth as part of an integrated whole. The Earth was seen to be an intelligent living being. In the Celtic lands of the British Isles and Northern Europe, she was revered as a life-giving goddess, providing us with all Five Elements essential for life's evolution: clean Air to breathe, pure Water, fertile Earth, transforming Fire and Spirit, the element which connects us to the invisible web of all life.

Our beautiful Earth has given us all so much to be thankful for. Our gratitude helps us to connect to the spiritual soul at the very core of our being. It is fuelled by Love and respect for the Earth and for all peoples, all creatures and each and every perfect micro-system. It brings awareness that we do not live separately from Nature. The Earth is our life's blood; each breath we take depends upon her, and now also on us, for we need to help the Earth to restore clean Air, clean Water and balanced ecosystems throughout the world. This is each and every person's basic birthright and responsibility.

We are at a critical time in the history of the Earth. We are emerging as a global community and we are all part of shaping the future we want for ourselves and for future generations. We are all responsible for creating a new future based on a culture of peace, universal human rights, economic justice and respect for all life on Earth.

We are developing a new awareness of our global responsibility and our connections to the Earth and to each other. We are becoming aware of ourselves as 'We'. This is a new evolutionary shift in consciousness. More and more people are identifying with this new 'We', this new sense of belonging to the global whole. We are moving towards sustainable systems that are life-enhancing and self-renewing. We are developing new industries that support the Earth, industries that are in harmony with the natural order and Nature's wisdom.

There is much in our world that does not follow this path. Anyone who cares deeply about the Earth and her people can become caught up in anger, resentment and great sadness. Our inability to stop the ruthless control of those in power creates circles of despair and powerlessness in our hearts. This is the 'us and them' mentality that has kept us fragmented for many generations.

When we become the collective 'We', we become a community of like minds, united in common heartfelt resolve. We inspire each other to believe that another world is possible. We become part of the change, the change of heart.

We are the people we are waiting for.

We are the people who care, who dare to question and dare to stand up for the Earth. We have a profound respect and compassion for the Earth and for all of life. We know in our hearts what is good and what is right. We follow our hearts and seek positive solutions based on Love, basic goodness and common sense. Supporting these changes is our common unity.

'Be the change you want to see happen.' Mahatma Gandhi

Changes of heart work by focusing on where we put our 'YES!'. Once we begin to live and work from a heart-centred reality, supporting and following our every 'Yes', the waves of our positive action spread and ripple through the whole of the intricate web of Life. We discover the most profound potential in the smallest of actions. Our actions today affect future generations and have far-reaching repercussions, creating ever-widening circles of positive change.

We are no longer living in isolated communities. We are no longer ignorant of the facts. We are each responsible for our own actions based on informed choice. The choices we make in our personal lives will affect and shape the bigger picture. By every act of personal beauty and loving response, by every act that is life-enhancing, we make a difference to the world. Our starting point is our immediate surroundings, our community, our friends and family, our work, our businesses and our power as consumers to support the products and businesses we wish to see prosper.

By our positive actions and acts of hope we inspire others to embrace our collective power and discover the profound potential of our collective identity. Once this is fully understood, we become different people. We learn to follow our hearts as well as our heads, doing what we know is right, trusting our intuition and becoming more fully integrated individuals. This is the inner evolution of the 'We' consciousness.

This place of integrated understanding is not imposed on us from the outside but created from the inside. We live as individuals, but feel and understand our connections to the whole of life. We become the individual within the collective.

Every single thing we do makes a difference.

We no longer see the Earth as something that serves us but begin to see how we can be of service to the Earth. This is a simple but major shift in consciousness that is necessary for the Earth's survival.

It is time for all of us to make changes about how we live our lives and to follow a path of the heart. By following our intuition and inspiration we encourage our own acts of heartfelt genius and boldness. This makes us feel alive and vital, gives us a great purpose and harnesses parts of ourselves we may have neglected or didn't even know we had. We no longer feel overwhelmed by the way the Earth's resources are managed, but recognize that change is in our hands, yours and mine, the hands of ordinary extraordinary people who have made a leap in understanding and are determined to make a difference.

We become part of the change by becoming part of the solution.

As ethical consumers we have great power to change the world economy from a power-over institution to one which supports local community, local produce, the life-enhancing production of goods, fairly traded goods, cooperatives, recycled products, food which is free of harmful chemicals, pesticides or genetic modification, and products that do not harm the Earth.

On a basic level, we are the consumers that the great commercial wheel serves. Our every purchase increases the availability of that product. So if you believe that it is wrong to exploit the men, women and children of the poorer countries, then as far as you can, buy fairly traded products. Your action then increases the availability of these products and supports a system that is generating goodwill and fairness. If you are against GM food, then buy organic food and increase the availability of food we can trust. This in turn supports small farmers and the availability of local produce and creates less demand for the agrochemicals that are destroying the balance of Nature.

Money is a kind of energy. Every single thing that our money buys supports that product. It supports the way that product was made, the people who were involved in making it and, unless it was produced by a cooperative or was fairly managed, it supports the person at the top who makes the most money. Consume less and consume consciously, with awareness of how each product came to you.

Live the life you feel good to live! Become the person you are proud to be! Every individual, organization, business and institution has a unique part to play. Once we reach critical mass, the gathering momentum will ensure that the Earth's future is safe.

All things are possible if we stand together.

Procrastination, excuses, fear of change, fear of not having enough money, fear of what others will think and say are some of the things that can stop us following our true heart's desire. None of them are helpful to us. We need to find out what is stopping us, draining us, restricting us, then how we can find ways to shift it so that we are free of all the restraints and blocks to our natural affinity for goodness and what feels right. But in many respects we do not need to dwell on past mistakes, just put ourselves back on track, re-establish our integrity and keep reaching for what we aspire to. It doesn't matter that we fail sometimes – what matters is that we try.

Each one of us adds to the world we create. Becoming conscious of this process changes our lives: how we live, think and interact with others.

The same law that creates our universe is operating throughout all of life. We are beginning to understand the nature of 'energy' and how everything we say, do and think has repercussions. We set off a chain of events by our every thought and deed. The energy we send out, we also receive. Expressing goodwill creates more goodwill. What comes round goes round. We create our world by what we give or what we take. Our giving creates open-hearted channels for Love and positive change, and for these things to come back to us. We create our own circles of energy, which have a profound effect on our everyday happiness and well-being.

At the root of old-style thinking lies warfare mentality. This warfare mindset, based on fear, scarcity, competition, the desire to dominate and to be in control, has led to the degeneration of the Earth's resources and her people. It is deeply rooted in the way we run our governments, our schools and our businesses, where killing off the competition is the goal. But change is happening. We are making a new commitment to make a difference rather than make a killing. We are creating a new set of values based on appreciation, sharing, collaboration, tolerance and cooperation.

Cooperation is the key to our survival. Wherever we see these seeds of hope it is crucial that we are proactive in supporting the changes.

Spirituality is moving from a conviction or belief to a lived reality that brings a heartfelt reverence and respect for all of life and all of the people of the Earth. Grassroots spirituality is growing out of our needs and the needs of the Earth. It is not being imposed on us. We are creating it ourselves. It is evolving and it is changing as our inner understanding grows. We are being guided by our inner wisdom, our integrity, our intuition and the wisdom of the Earth. We trust ourselves to do what is right with instinctive sureness. It is the path of the heart, of Love, compassion, forgiveness, tolerance, sharing and gratitude. It is not complex or elaborate. It is very simple. All the great spiritual teachers from all the world's religions have told us the same thing: we must find our hearts and then we will find our true way.

Spirituality is not a religion. It is a journey and an inner connection. For some of us it is a natural part of our way of being and living, but for others it sometimes takes a crisis to bring changes of outlook and lifestyle. Illness, for example, can be viewed as a positive experience, an open door that invites us to change. We can take the opportunity to leave behind our old patterns and embrace new ways to live and relate. But why wait for a crisis? By becoming more committed to our own spiritual journey, a whole new world opens up for us.

Each of us has the power to change. It is up to each of us to live with this possibility and to inspire others to make that shift in perception. The changes we make on the inside have far-reaching repercussions in the outer world. Harmony on the inside creates harmony on the outside and is reflected in all we do.

A necessary working part of our whole self is our intuition. This faculty is inherent in all of us. We have been encouraged not to trust it and yet it is an essential lifeline, a vital asset. For too long we have neglected to appreciate it. This gift is life-given, but blocked by decades of fear, mistrust and lack of use.

If you are not used to acting on your intuition, you often barely notice when you have an insight and disregard it if you do. Yet how often in hindsight do you wish you had acted on that flash of intuition? Despite centuries of social taboo, our sixth sense remains as bright and accessible as ever. We only have to acknowledge it is there and it is at our service, as it always has been, an integral part of our whole self.

Experiencing deep heartfelt connections to the Earth will bring us closer to understanding ourselves and trusting our intuition. It will help us to foster a sense of belonging and Love for the Earth and all peoples of the Earth.

To live in harmony with the Earth, we need to remember our connection to her. This book is dedicated to rediscovering and reawakening the journey of Love and respect for the awesome Wonder that is our Earth. In our hearts we then feel true inhabitants of our wonderful unique planet. We feel connected on all levels of our being. We rediscover the sacred in ourselves and in all that surrounds us.

Silver
Birch

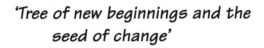

Betula pendula

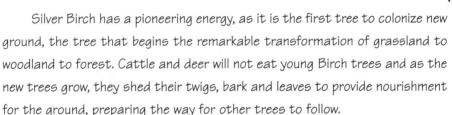

'Tree of new beginnings and the seed of change'

Silver Birch has a pioneering energy, as it is the first tree to colonize new ground, the tree that begins the remarkable transformation of grassland to woodland to forest. Cattle and deer will not eat young Birch trees and as the new trees grow, they shed their twigs, bark and leaves to provide nourishment for the ground, preparing the way for other trees to follow.

In the Celtic Tree Ogham, a system that links different qualities to each of the native trees, the Birch is the first tree and represents new beginnings, birth, nourishment and cleansing.

Astrologically, it is ruled by the Moon, which enhances intuition, by Venus, which brings Love, and by Jupiter, which creates good fortune and happiness. Silver Birch is known as 'Lady of the Woods'. This graceful tree is seen at its best on a moonlit night or glowing pink in the light of the setting Sun or the sunrise. It brings a light airy presence wherever it grows.

It is a short-lived tree, usually living for 80–100 years and growing to 20–30 feet. The roots are near the surface and they prefer light dry soils. The sparse foliage allows other things to grow beneath the tree and the beautiful heart-shaped leaves cling to the branches long into the Winter months. Despite its delicate appearance, Birch is very hardy and can grow high up in the mountains and tolerate extremes of cold.

In April the male and female catkins can be seen growing on the same branch. Fruiting catkins stay on the tree until Winter, when they break up into scales and winged wind-borne seeds.

Growing Silver Birch Trees

Silver Birch trees are easy to grow. Place the mature catkins in a brown paper bag in the Autumn and allow them to dry out. Sort out the seeds and sow them immediately. Cover them with a layer of sharp sand and leave them outside over the Winter until they germinate the following Spring. When they are large enough, plant them out into their permanent sites in the Autumn and Winter months.

Folklore and Legend

Silver Birch twigs are associated with purity and cleansing and were used in the past to beat out negative influences and prepare the way for renewal. Criminals were thought to have come under the influence of bad spirits and were 'birched' as an act of cleansing. Land boundaries were beaten with Birch twigs every year to drive out the spirits of the old year and to clear out any energy that might have become stuck there.

Birch is dedicated to the Norse Goddess Freya or Frigga, who is associated with Love and love-making. It was an old Welsh custom for a couple to exchange Birch twigs in the Spring as a symbol of their Love. Bundles of Birch twigs were given to couples on their wedding day to ensure fertility.

The Wisdom of Silver Birch

The pioneering energy of the Silver Birch inspires us to begin new ventures and to follow our visions. By doing something that will bring positive change into our lives and into the world, we prepare the way for new directions. Our pioneering spirit will inspire others to follow our lead and from small beginnings we can create big changes, just as a huge forest begins with the first young Silver Birch trees.

The Silver Birch sheds its twigs, bark and leaves, teaching us to let go of unwanted aspects of our lives and selves so that we are free to move forward into a new beginning. New growth and new directions are nourished by our experiences, so let go of the past lovingly and with thanks, then look for the chance openings that will help you to move on. Welcome change into your life!

Change does not happen all at once, but the first thing you do will open the way for the next to follow. Do one thing at a time. Better to begin in small loving ways than not to begin at all.

Let the Silver Birch's pliant twigs and heart-shaped leaves inspire you to let go of all worry and stress, to dance with the winds of change and to follow your heart.

The Wood and Its Uses

Birch has a heavy pale wood used for barrel-making, tool handles and furniture. Traditionally babies' cradles were made of Birch and any carving of Birch wood makes an ideal gift for a baby. A healing wand of Birch will help focus any new start or new project.

Oil made from Birch bark is used in tanning leather. Birch bark is water-resistant and contains large amounts of resin. In the past it was used for roofing, shoes and leggings, for making canoes, in basket making and for parchment and paper making.

Birch twigs are used to make brooms. To make a Birch brush, gather freshly dropped or cut twigs and bind the ends together with strong natural string. Tie a loop at the end of the string so that you can hang it up. Alternatively, drive a long stake through your tied bundle (traditionally Ash, Willow or Hazel) for a more traditional besom broom.

Herbal and Edible Uses: *Betula pendula*

Sap
Traditionally the tree was tapped in March for the syrup, which was used as a sugar. It was also used to make Birch sap wine, which was drunk as a Spring tonic.

Young Leaves

Collect the young leaves in late Spring and early Summer and dry them in brown paper bags. Use an infusion of the leaves (see page 35) as a gentle sedative, to break up kidney stones or gallstones and as a mouthwash for sore mouths. Birch leaves are a tonic, an antiseptic, a diuretic and an effective remedy for cystitis and other infections of the urinary system. The young leaves can be used to make wine.

Bark

Collect small patches of bark in early Spring. It will ease muscle pain if applied externally. Apply the fresh wet inside of the bark directly to the skin.

Important: As with all trees, when taking the bark, remove it in small patches. Be careful not to remove it in a continuous ring around the trunk or the tree will die. This is called 'ringing the tree'.

Twigs

Birch twigs are used in Scandinavian countries in the sauna or sweat lodge as a cleanser. The body is gently beaten with the twigs to increase the circulation and to help release toxins from the skin.

Spring Cleansing Tonic

1. Break a handful of Birch twigs and unopened buds into a jug.
2. Fill with boiling water, cover and leave overnight.
3. Drink the next day.
4. Top up with more boiling water and drink the new mixture the following day.
5. Continue doing this for several days.

Silver Birch Essential Oil

Add a few drops to a tablespoon of almond oil and use as a soothing massage oil that will ease muscle pain.

Healing Properties

Birch brings boldness to our actions and helps us to give birth to new ideas. Whatever you want to do, clear the way. Prepare to make changes in your life.

As part of your preparation, nourish yourself and those around you. The Love you put into motion now will ensure that you are on the right path and that good will grow from the changes you will make.

Find the time to go for a walk in Birch woods and sit with Birch trees. If you live in a town or city, find a local Birch tree to sit with. The Birch brings a special calmness and uplifting energy. Pick some twigs, with respect and Love for the tree. Place them in a vase of Water and have them near you. Bring the energy of the Silver Birch and the Spirit of the woodland into your life.

Use Birch twigs for purification, cleansing and renewal. Use them to clear away what has become stuck or stagnant in your life. Sweep around yourself with a bunch of Birch twigs to clear stuck emotions and revitalize yourself. Do this every day until you begin to feel clearer and able to move on.

Spirit of Birch

The Gifts of the Earth

The great wealth of trees and vegetation that covers the Earth allows us to live and breathe on this wondrous planet. The sheer abundance of vegetation that the Earth is capable of producing means that there is always more than enough to share. With careful planting and watering, even a desert can soon be transformed into a productive forest, creating its own self-regulating ecosystem. Life here on Earth yearns to express its abundance, its fertility and ability to reproduce itself. Each perfect flower and each perfect seed is an expression of that abundance.

Each time we engage with Nature we have the opportunity to experience our feelings of reverence for life. When we open our hearts to the world of wonder and beauty around us, we are opening ourselves to our receptivity and natural spirituality. Experiencing the gifts of the Earth will take us on a journey of self-discovery and bring us unforgettable moments of communion and spiritual nourishment.

Life-Giving Trees

Trees have been described as the lungs of the Earth. These gentle strong lifeforms, along with other plants, give us the oxygen-rich air we need to breathe. Their breath gives us life and we owe them our gratitude, our recognition and our respect for the part they play in our very existence.

Trees are a living presence and we can all sense their energy, which helps us to feel our connection to all living things. They are, like the Earth, all-giving, asking for nothing in return. Through their beauty we are uplifted and with each seasonal change they bring us delight.

The 'Tree Tribes', 'the Standing Ones', as they were once known, were once the dominant lifeform on the Earth, covering huge areas of land. After the last Ice Age they flourished and adapted, creating perfection for themselves and consequently for the human tribes, animals, birds, insects and reptiles that lived among them.

Today, their breathing allows us to breathe; their fruit, seeds and nuts give us food to eat; their timber helps us to keep warm and build our homes, other buildings, tools and transport. They also provide us with other products on which our prosperity has grown, such as medicines and paper.

Trees teach us about the importance of renewal as they shed their leaves and seeds, their outer achievements, and find strength and vitality through a period of rest in the dark of the year.

They teach us stillness and about slowing down to find contentment within.

They show us the importance of strong roots to maintain stability.

Trees were once respected and thanked for their gifts, but modern commercial agriculture has lost touch with the spirit of gratitude and respect for the balance of Nature. Forest clearance destroys the natural habitat of many creatures as trees are ripped from the land and soil is washed away, leaving land that takes years to regenerate. Dense plantations for the timber trade and paper industry support much less wildlife than natural forests and are a soul-less environment for the trees to live in. Both industries are managed purely for commercial gain and show little understanding of our interdependency or any respect for the trees.

We are destroying the lungs of the Earth as we destroy the forests.

Tree Planting
Planting trees to replace all those that have been taken is a huge task,

but we have to begin somewhere. Plant trees wherever you can in your locality. Plant commemorative trees to celebrate a birth, to mark a death, to honour a friendship, for hope and for our grandchildren. Plant trees to mark special occasions. Plant more orchards. Plant more hedgerows. Plant more trees! Every tree that we plant is a gift for the future.

Tree planting brings life-sustaining changes on many levels. Places that are now barren, which support very little wildlife or food, can be transformed by planting trees. We can support tree-planting programmes and initiatives by donating our time, energy and funds (see Networking Solutions). We can also begin our own projects by involving our local community in creating new local woodlands for the future. Support for any tree-planting initiative means we are giving something back to the Earth.

Recycling paper and using recycled paper products also help to reduce the damage that continues to be done. We can be more proactive in this by only buying recycled paper products and encouraging our workplaces, governments and schools to do the same.

Tree Spirits or Dryads

Trees are seen as living beings that span the Five Elements. Their branches are in the Air, they take their energy from Fire (the Sun), their roots are deep within the Earth and they drink from the living Waters of the Earth. They also inhabit the world of the fifth element, Spirit, and we are all able to communicate with them on this level.

We also have a wealth of tree myths, tree legends and tree lore preserved for us in our folksongs and folktales, which show us that our ancestors had a deep relationship with the trees.

It was once commonly understood all over the world that the tangible presence of a tree was due to the existence of a Spirit within it. The Druids called them 'the Many-Eyed Ones' or 'the Hooded Ones' and believed that they watched and recorded the comings and goings of the human race, passing on their impartial observations to the cosmic memory banks that exist outside our time. Important meetings were held under large trees with this in mind. Kings were crowned, laws passed and people executed there. Public events such as marriages and courts were held. Trees were planted at crossroads, to mark boundaries and at significant points on the land.

A Tree Spirit, or Dryad, can be understood as a huge energy field radiating out from each tree. In large old trees it can radiate for several miles. It is possible to make contact with a Dryad, though this is much easier in Spring and Summer, when the trees are growing and active, than in Autumn and Winter, when their energy drops down into the Earth for rest and renewal.

Within a wood or forest each Dryad will interconnect and overlap with several other Dryads, all occupying the same space without any trouble. The wisdom of the Dryad remains constant no matter what age the tree, but old trees have a deeper understanding of their wisdom, like any elder. If a tree subdivides, the wisdom of the original tree is complete and transfers in its entirety. The subdivision needs something to anchor itself to and this is usually a new seedling or a cutting that grows roots and becomes a new tree. Sometimes a Tree Spirit will agree to subdivide into a token piece of wood, a wand or staff and will form a working partnership with the higher self of the human who carries it about. In this way the Dryad greatly amplifies and guides the inner wisdom and psychic abilities of its carrier and gains for itself the mobility that it lacked as a tree. This is the origin of the staff or wand carried by a wise woman, holy man or healer. Through the wisdom and abilities of the Dryad, the human will have a more developed connection to the Spirit realms and greater healing power. Wood that holds a resident Dryad is called 'livewood' and has a very different feel from other wood.

Most Dryads are, however, not interested in humans. We move too fast for one thing and they tend to ignore us unless we are looking for contact with them or mean them harm.

If a person intends to cut down a tree or any part of a tree, the Tree Spirit withdraws, allowing the wood to die. It does, however, retain some of the qualities of the original tree in it and for this reason we like the living feel of wood and touch wood for luck.

Communicating with Trees

Opening ourselves to the wisdom of the trees is to experience the interconnectedness of all things. By getting to know trees and communicating with them on a spiritual level, we are getting to know ourselves.

If you are drawn towards a tree, then make the time to slow down and make contact with it. Approach slowly, feeling how you can reach out to another being without words. Open your heart to the tree in loving gratitude for its beautiful presence and gifts. Moving slowly towards it, stop when you feel you should and wait until you feel that it is the right moment to move closer. You may feel it is right to circle the tree at a distance, moving sunwise to indicate you are part of the natural order. You may find yourself spiralling slowly in towards the centre. Picture the tree having several layers of energy and see if you can feel yourself moving through these as you get closer to the tree. The final layer is within its bark as you reach out to the energy at the heart of the tree.

Make physical contact with the tree by resting your brow or your spine against its trunk or by sitting next to it or putting your arms around it. Do whatever feels natural at the time. Slowly drop your energy from your head and take it right down into the Earth. Feel yourself developing a strong root system and becoming anchored to the Earth. In this way you become more in tune with the energy of the tree. Feel the stability you gain from forming a strong root system. Let the energy of the Earth flow through you, giving you nourishment, stillness and a strong centre.

Stay connected in this way until you feel the moment has changed and then ask the tree if you may share its wisdom. Meditate with the tree until you feel complete and then thank the tree for sharing itself with you before slowly making a move.

If you would like to cut a staff or wand from the tree, ask out loud or send a thought message to it and wait to feel a response. Most trees are totally generous with their wood, especially if it is for any spiritual use.

Trees are intrinsically a generous tribe and the more we learn to appreciate them, the easier it becomes to form links and friendships with them. We must, however, slow down considerably, allowing them to register our presence and our wish to communicate. With trees we should never be rushed or expect them to rush. We have to learn how to listen and how to drop our energy into theirs. Each species of tree has its own particular overall energy pattern. Within this, individual trees also have their own personalities. Trees communicate. They do not like to be ignored and would rather we communicate back!

The old tales advise us to leave a gift for the tree. I feel that our Love and gratitude is the gift that trees really appreciate, but we can also be of service to them by making a pledge to protect them. This might include political action or eco-activism, protecting trees as well as growing and planting them wherever we can. We can also be of service to individual trees by watering young trees in dry weather and clearing rubbish from around them. Many small copses and woods are used for dumping rubbish, but we can help to preserve them as places of beauty and spiritual renewal, places of sanctuary in which Nature and wildlife can flourish.

After spending time with a tree, make an offering at its base by creating a pattern or mandala (a circular pattern) out of the leaves, seeds, stones and twigs you find there. As you create it, link to the Spirit of the tree and the Spirits of the land. Sing to them. Open your heart in loving gratitude.

Sacred Groves

A sacred grove is a special place to gather, to be with the Spirit of Nature and to connect to your own spirituality. It consists of a group of trees normally in a circle with an open space in the middle. Groves are open to the elements and to the sky so that we experience Nature all around us. They provide a community space for ceremonies to celebrate the seasonal flow of the Earth's cycles and a personal place for contemplation and ritual.

In the past a sacred grove would have consisted only of native trees, chosen for their special energies and wisdom: Oak, Hazel, Rowan, Holly, Yew, Elder, Crab Apple, Alder, Hawthorn, Blackthorn, Silver Birch, Willow and Ash. The arrangement, location and numbers of trees would vary, but there would have been a deep connection to the Spirit of the place through the Earth energies present. It may be that these sacred groves weren't planted at all, but were thinned from self-seeded trees that were already growing on a special site.

If you have land or woodland, you could create your own sacred grove. Tune in to the Spirit of the land and the trees and follow an intuitive path to find the best place for this special site. Consider the 'atmosphere', how a particular spot makes you feel. Check this out with other people who know the land. As well as this, there are practical considerations of privacy and ease of access, especially for wheelchairs. Consider how the land drains in the Winter and avoid areas likely to become waterlogged and muddy. Groves are best when their use is integrated into daily life and for this reason they should be located within walking distance of a house or communal building.

The Spirit of Vegetation

By eating plants we are linked to the complete growth cycle of life on Earth. Since plants photosynthesize using the energy of sunlight (and to some extent moonlight), when we take in the energy of the plant as we eat it, we take in the energy of the Sun and the Moon as well. Since plants draw up their nourishment from the Earth and the Waters of the Earth, we also take in the Earth's goodness and nourishment as we eat them. They are a bridge between the world of Nature and the world that we create for ourselves here on Earth.

Plants, like trees, have a wealth of healing properties and symbolic meanings handed down through the green language of our folklore and folk customs. We give flowers, for example, as gifts of friendship, to the sick, as expressions of Love, as a mark of respect for the dead and to celebrate new life. There is joy in their energy. They open our hearts to our spirituality and to a deep connection to the Earth.

When we work with plants by growing them in our gardens or by gathering some of our own food or medicine from the wild, we are participating in Nature. We are experiencing her, delighting in her, interacting with her, learning and finding Oneness within ourselves. If we develop this relationship in ways that create heartfelt gratitude, we no longer just take. We become sensitive to the needs of the natural world and we learn how to give something back.

Learning to recognize, use and grow edible and medicinal plants gives us a deep connection to the Earth. We are no longer separated from her. She is our provider, our friend, giver of life, Mother Earth, and we are part of her living presence each time we eat from her bountiful store.

Medicinal Herbs

Each plant species has its own vibration, force, personality or 'signature' and this is the healing energy of the plant. In the 1500s, Paracelsus, a Swiss physician and alchemist, developed what he called the 'doctrine of signatures'. He observed that the plants gave signals to help humans discover their medicinal uses and the essential energy of the plant was reflected in the way it looked and grew. This seemed improbable to many, but the herbal uses Paracelsus proposed have been verified by modern medical research.

Medicinal and edible herbs are mostly our wild native plants, not the cultivated ones, and their history goes back a long way. With the advent of 'tidy' gardens and flower gardens they became known as weeds. Weeds are, for me, the most interesting plants in a garden, as they almost always have an energetic, herbal, medicinal or culinary use. I grow cultivated vegetables and culinary herbs, but I also cultivate the wild plants that I can eat or use for medicine. Because they are natives they are very hardy and even in Winter I can find some salad or one of the old 'pot-herbs' to eat when all the cultivated vegetables and leaves are finished. Weeding then becomes harvesting!

Herbal remedies do not just work on the level of curing the physical illness, but also on the subtle energy fields of our bodies, our emotional and spiritual selves. They also have an impact on our life force, our vital energy that brings good health and equilibrium both within and without. This vital force helps the body to harness its own healing power and to aid its own healing process. Once activated, the power of the body's lifeforce can bring about miracles of healing. Plants can act as a catalyst to this inner healing power.

Collecting and Drying Herbs

Harvest herbs when they are at their peak. Leaves are at their prime before the flowers fully form. Flowers are at their prime just before and as they begin to open fully. Roots are best picked in Autumn, when the goodness is passed back down from the leaves. Whenever possible, pick the aerial parts when the Moon is waxing to full and the roots as the Moon is waning. Before you pick anything, always thank the plant for its gift. This open-hearted gratitude will greatly help in the healing process.

Pick herbs on a sunny day, after the dew has dried. Avoid picking plants near roadsides, on old industrial sites, under electricity pylons, from land that has been sprayed with chemical fertilizers or from private land without permission. It is also illegal to pick from protected natural sites.

A good rule when harvesting plants is to leave an area looking as if it has not been picked over. Choose the finest plants and cut them randomly with secateurs or scissors. Place them loosely either in an open basket or head first into brown paper bags. Tie up the bag and create a loop in the string for a carrying handle. On your return home, sort through them, discarding any that are marked or eaten by insects. Return them to the brown paper bag and hang them up to dry in a warm airy place out of the sunlight.

When the herbs are completely dry, store them in dark jars or clean brown paper bags, as light will destroy their beneficial properties.

People often worry about dosage with herbs or about picking the wrong plant. I think it is important that you do not use herbs if you are imparting any worries into them. This will block their energies and may even bring some harm. If you are a beginner, start with familiar herbs. All the culinary herbs have herbal uses, so build up your confidence using these familiar plants and then go on to use familiar native plants.

Dosage Guidelines
Whenever possible, use herbs freshly picked so that their vital energy is strong. Obviously a store of dried herbs is good for Winter use. Dried herbs are more concentrated, so you use fewer of them.

✎ For a single dose, add 1 cup of water to 3 teaspoons or 1 tablespoon of fresh herb or 1 teaspoon of dried herb (3 teaspoons or 1 tablespoon of fresh herb = 1 teaspoon of dried herb).

✎ You can also make a pint of the mixture at a time. Use 15g–25g of dried herb to 570ml of water / $^1/_2$–1 ounce of dried herb to 1 pint of water (two to three times more of the fresh herb is needed). Drink some hot and keep the rest in the fridge. Drink cold from a wineglass.

✎ Generally take your herbal preparation three times a day, perhaps more frequently at first if a symptom is more acute. (An acute illness arises suddenly and intensely. A chronic illness develops slowly and continues for a long time or is constantly recurring.) Large doses do not necessarily work better; a slower healing process is often more thorough.

You have to use a common-sense approach with herbs. For the very young, elderly or the weak, use fewer herbs. The golden rule is: *If in doubt, don't!*

It is generally recommended to use a herb or combination of herbs for no more than 12 weeks because of the dangers of certain chemicals building up in the system.

Herbal Preparations

Herbs can be used in a variety of ways. We can absorb them by drinking herb teas or by eating them. They can also be absorbed through the skin via bathing or footbaths. They can be applied directly onto the skin as a poultice. Common preparations are infusions and decoctions.

An infusion or tisane (*soft aerial parts/leaves/flowers*): This is simply made by pouring boiling water over the herbs. Cover to keep in all the essential oils, leave for 10 minutes and strain off the leaves and drink.

A decoction (*berries/bark/roots/seeds*): Chop or crush the parts, put in a pan and bring to the boil. Simmer for 10 or 15 minutes. Alternatively, you can pour on cold water and leave to stand overnight, before straining off the herbs before drinking.

A compress: Herbal infusions and decoctions can also be used as a compress by soaking a piece of cotton cloth in the solution and applying it warm to the skin. It can be covered with a towel or plastic to keep the heat and the moisture in.

A poultice: To make a poultice, mash or crush the plant to a pulp with a little boiling water. Place it directly where it is needed, with a little olive oil or thin muslin to protect the skin and help removal of the herb.

Flower Essences

Flower essences are created using sunlight and spring water to extract the essential energy of a plant from the flowers. They act on the emotional level and can help to bring change by balancing mental and emotional disharmony. Often this is the root cause of an illness. Flower remedies can also be used to prevent illness from developing by restoring inner harmony (*see page 212*).

Communication with the Spirits of Plants

In just the same way that we can communicate with a tree, so we can communicate with plants. They have a gentle, subtle energy, but it will begin to reveal itself to us if we develop the art of inner listening.

If you are drawn towards a plant, herb or flower, then take heed of this and follow it up in any way that appeals to you. Meditate next to the plant, reaching out with your senses to make contact and intuitively receive impressions from it. If you are using plants as part of your healing process, welcome the plant and its energy by making a connection to the living plant if possible. If this is not possible, at least familiarize yourself with what it looks like from a book, create a picture-link in your mind between the plant and yourself and always send it your thanks. This will open the channels for you to receive its healing qualities. Plant it in your garden or window box or grow it from seed, so that you become linked to it in a very direct way.

Healing Cycles

The energy shift that you gain from working with a plant will filter into all aspects of your life: how you relate to others, how you approach life itself. This is a gentle process, like the plants themselves. It is not the instant hit of modern allopathic medicine. This might cure the manifested illness, but often it leaves the cause of the problem still in place.

When taking a herb, especially if you do understand the vibrational shift it is capable of, be proactive. Do what needs to be done to change the things that are not helping your illness. Every little thing helps, so if your energy is low, just do one small thing at a time. Everything in Nature works in cycles and this includes the healing process. Healing is not linear. It is aided by many factors and each small change gradually creates more beneficial cycles.

The power of your intent will have a profound impact on your life force. The power of your Love is equally transformative. The vibration of Love dispels harmful negative vibrations and is a harmonizing force that brings healing. Love yourself, be good to yourself and give yourself what you know you need for health and harmony. Reverse negative and destructive thoughts by sending out Love and gratitude. Replace dissatisfaction with a desire to create positive solutions. Happiness and laughter are great healers, so follow the threads that lead to your happiness.

The Ogham

The Ogham (pronounced 'Oh am') system was an early alphabet used by the Druids and the Celtic people. The Ogham script is written vertically and consists of groups of short horizontal or diagonal lines crossing a central stem line to represent each letter. It is read from the bottom up and each letter is also a sound, a magical invocation, and has its own spiritual meaning.

Although the Druids did not write down their knowledge, the early Christian monks were avid collators of information and recorded some of the Druidic teachings. In two medieval manuscripts, the *Book of Ballymote*, written in 1391, and the *Book of Lecan*, written in 1416, the symbols and meanings of a Tree Ogham, a Flower Ogham and a Bird Ogham were recorded. These manuscripts concerned themselves with these Oghams' use as an alphabet system, but there are also elaborate and poetic descriptions within each classification which give clues to their deeper spiritual significance.

The Oghams were used by the Druids to classify, memorize and store information. This could then be used to encode deeper levels of spiritual wisdom and understand abstract concepts. An Ogham symbol works in the same way as an astrological symbol – once you build up knowledge of the energy that it represents, you are capable of understanding a huge amount from one small pictogram. Before the use of the written word this must have been a very useful tool for communication, magic and healing.

Ogham symbols can be found carved on stones in Wales, Southern Ireland and Scotland, along with many other symbols that make up this early form of written language. The stones were all carved between AD 300 and 700 and may have been marker stones for boundaries or funerary stones for the dead.

The Tree Ogham

The Tree Ogham is an example of an ancient wisdom that has been slowly re-emerging and organically growing over the last 50 years. It is a link between the living traditions of the past and the evolving traditions of the present and provides us with both an inner language of symbols we can use and a deep connection to the trees.

The Tree Ogham system is a means of communication through each of the 20 Ogham symbols that are carved onto Ogham sticks or staves. Each symbol, called a *fedha* or *few*, represents a tree or shrub and its underlying energy or wisdom. It can be written alone or combined to create a larger picture.

The 20 Ogham Fedha or Fews
(read from the bottom upwards)

10	APPLE	Q. Queirt
9	HAZEL	C. Coll
8	HOLLY	T. Tinne
7	OAK	D. Duir
6	HAWTHORN	H. Huath

20	YEW	I. Idhadh
19	ASPEN	E. Eadhadh
18	HEATHER	U. Ur
17	GORSE	O. Onn
16	FIR	A. Ailm

5	ASH	N. Nion
4	WILLOW	S. Saille
3	ALDER	F. Fearn
2	ROWAN	L. Luis
1	BIRCH	B. Beithe

15	ELDER	R. Ruis
14	BLACKTHORN	St/z. Straiph
13	BROOM	nG. nGetal
12	IVY	G. Gort
11	VINE	m. Muin

Making Your Own Set of Ogham Sticks or Staves

Collecting a piece of wood from each of the trees in the Ogham system gives us a unique opportunity to tune into each of the trees separately, understand their different energies and build up personal relationships with them.

You can create your own set of Ogham staves by communicating with each tree in turn and intuitively asking for a twig to use for this purpose. You may prefer not to cut living wood but to wait until the tree sheds some wood naturally. If you do decide to use fallen wood it must be fairly fresh. Old wood is likely to have beetle in it and it is not strong.

Each stick holds the imprint and qualities of each tree within it. Mark each one with its Ogham symbol, carving or painting it on in whatever way feels good to you.

It is also acceptable to create a set of Ogham sticks using the wood from one tree only, marked with the different symbols to represent the different trees. This type of set may have been traditionally made out of Rowan, Hazel or Yew because of these trees' links to divination or the Otherworld, but none have survived for us to see.

Each set of Ogham sticks is a personal expression of the person who makes it, so create your own in whatever way feels right to you. You may choose to collect only from trees that grow in a significant or sacred place, where the Earth energies feel potent. You may decide to only collect the wood at the full Moon or at dawn. Do whatever feels right for you and follow your intuition.

Talismans and Healing Wands

You can also make yourself a talisman or healing wand by carving an Ogham symbol onto a piece of wood to wear around your neck or to carry in your pocket. This sets up a sympathetic resonance between you, the symbol and energetic healing qualities of the tree. It also helps to remind you of the connection, your understanding of it and what strength you are drawing from it each time you see or touch it. For example, you may feel you need the strength and courage of Oak to help you, so you carry a small piece of Oak in your pocket or an Oak wand. You can also combine several Ogham symbols together along a central stem line to create a beneficial blend of energy.

Using the Ogham for Guidance and Healing

You can use your Ogham in many ways as you work with the wisdom of the trees. It acts as a bridge between our conscious minds and the world of Spirit. It is a means of communicating with our own inner wisdom, our intuition and our Spirit guides. It can be used as a focus for healing or for guidance.

- 🌲 To use the Ogham for divination or guidance, begin with a short meditation. Connect to the Oneness of all of life.

- 🌲 Then focus on what you want to ask and choose intuitively from your set of Ogham staves. You can choose one stick only for a broad overview or you can choose three sticks for a more detailed understanding.

- 🌲 Lay them out before you and interpret them in the light of each other. Lay them out as illustrated overleaf:

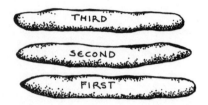

1. The first represents the underlying root of the situation.
2. The second represents the material world, the present moment caught in time. Interpret it in relation to the first.
3. The third stick is the most fluid and represents the world of Spirit where all possibilities exist. It will help guide your actions towards the most positive outcome.

Understanding grows with time and experience. The more you work with trees and spend time with them, the more you will learn of their wisdom. Choose an Ogham stick at each new Moon and explore your connection and understanding during the month until the next new Moon. Keep a record of your observations in a notebook, recording your insights and journey with the trees.

If you are drawn towards the energy of certain trees, spend as much time as you can with the trees themselves. Learn about them from them: how they grow, the shape of their leaves and flowers, what their habits are, their favoured habitat, their herbal healing properties, their culinary uses or their other uses. This helps us to understand their essential energy and to form lasting friendships with them.

At the end of each chapter in this book you will find a tree, its Ogham symbol, its herbal and healing properties and the underlying energy of its deep spiritual wisdom.

Genetically Modified Plants

Nature is a beautifully organized complex system. Genes function as part of an integrated whole. Despite the biotech industry's clumsy attempts to portray genetic manipulation of plants as natural and unthreatening extensions of natural breeding, the truth is that gene technology is being used to create huge accelerated changes that could not occur naturally. There are so many 'unknowns' that the risks to health and the environment are unquantifiable. The genes and the proteins that are being manipulated do not work in isolation but have evolved to exist and function in groups, as part of a complex connected whole. The same genes in their natural groupings have been finely tuned to work harmoniously together by millions of years of evolution.

Nature has established boundaries so that reproduction can normally take place only between closely related forms. This means that naturally speaking, a tomato plant cannot cross-pollinate with a cabbage plant, and so on. Genetic modification brings about combinations of genes that would never occur naturally. A gene from a common soil bacterium has been transferred to soya beans to make them resistant to a herbicide; anti-freeze protein genes from an arctic fish have been introduced into tomatoes and potatoes to confer resistance to frost. Plants have been modified to last longer, look different or taste better and to be tolerant of large amounts of weedkiller and insecticide, which would otherwise kill them. This potentially means an increase in productivity, but farmers who have been growing GM crops in North America, Canada and Argentina are reporting greater dependency on herbicides and pesticides as new weed problems are emerging and insect pests are gaining resistance.

The artificial nature of genetic modification does not automatically make it dangerous. It is the unpredictability of how the foreign gene will behave in its new host that is worrying. Further cause for concern is the risk these rogue genes and proteins will pose to our health when these modified plants get into our food chain. There is a lot of medical concern that their unpredictability will lead to new allergies, antibiotic resistance, damage to our immune systems, damage to our vital organs and an increase in cancer.

These genetically engineered or transgenic plants are now proven to affect and cross-pollinate with other species in the environment in which they are grown. Contamination is inevitable and directly threatens our rich heritage of wild plants, our insects, especially the bees, the birds that feed on the insects, the predators that feed on the birds, and so on throughout the ecosystem.

We are the consumers who will let this happen or stop it happening.

We must insist that all food products be labelled to show GM ingredients so that consumers can make an informed choice. We must let our supermarkets know that we will not buy products containing GM ingredients, pressure the government to become a GM-free country and support the larger national campaigns, such as those of Greenpeace, which are working to raise public awareness.

Our most positive action is to support organic farming by only buying organic food and organic products. This is the food we can trust, grown without harmful pesticides, herbicides, chemical fertilizers or GM seed. It is grown in harmony with Nature, with respect for all life and by people who care about the Earth.

Elder

Sambucus nigra

'Tree of regeneration and wisdom'

Elder is a very approachable and generous tree that readily shares its gifts with humankind. Anyone who is interested in gathering food and medicine will sing the praises of this little tree that gives so much. Every part of the Elder is useful for something, except for firewood. Country lore tells us never to burn the wood of Elder. (It doesn't burn well anyway and the central pith hole makes a good habitat for insects.) People of the past would never senselessly cut down the Elder, because it is a good hedgerow tree and its medicinal and edible value was important.

Elder is the 15th tree of the Celtic Tree Ogham, representing renewal, regeneration and transformation from within. It is associated with Venus, the wisdom of the feminine principle and the cauldron of rebirth.

Plant an Elder in the corner of your garden. It is not a big tree and it brings a very special energy. In the past it was considered to bring protection if planted near the house. At Midsummer it will provide you with flowers for herb teas, Elderflower cordial and Elderflower champagne. In the Autumn it is laden with berries for jam, mixed fruit pies, rich dark berry drinks and wine.

Elder is a very fast-growing tree and in a garden you will need to cut it back from time to time. This is a great opportunity to practise your skills of communicating with trees! Take your time! Slow down! Thank the tree for its presence and gifts and explain what you are doing. Doing this helps us to express our Love and respect for the tree.

Growing Elder Trees

Elder roots easily from any of its parts and because of this it is known as a tree of regeneration. New trees can be grown from its seeds but are easily grown from cuttings.

Trees from Cuttings

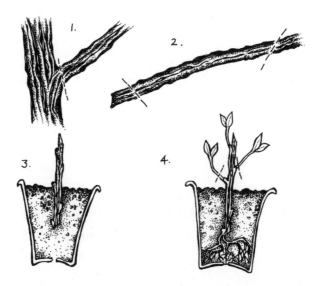

In the Autumn simply cut some of the small twigs, cut them into pieces and put them straight into the earth or bunch them together in a plant pot filled with good compost. By the Spring they will have rooted. Cut off all but one of the new shoots and remove any flowers that develop in the first season. The young Elders can be planted out in the following Autumn.

Folklore and Legend

There is a wealth of folklore, legend and history that portrays the Elder tree as a powerful female energy of great wisdom. Known as the 'Queen of the Trees' and 'the Witches' tree', the Elder has the calm wise energy of a Grandmother, Crone, elder or wise woman. She was feared as well as respected, for it was believed that she could wreak havoc if angered or offended. If an Elder needs to be cut back, let the tree know first and work with respect for its life force. If it is to be cut down completely, well, you had better have a good reason!

The Wisdom of the Elder

The ease with which the Elder regenerates helps us to understand the natural process of regeneration. There is always a beginning in every ending and always an end in every beginning. If you fully experience the end and then let it go and move on, then you open the way for new beginnings, new growth. If you don't begin, you never have the experience. Through this we learn to keep moving, integrating our experiences into our understanding. For it is through experience that we learn, grow wise, become respected elders. The wisdom of the Elder helps us to integrate our cycles of death and rebirth and to count our blessings as we move from one phase to the next.

The Wood and Its Uses

Elder is a hard close-grained yellow wood which polishes up well with a little beeswax polish. The bigger pieces can be used for carving.

If you do need to cut an Elder, then use the wood if possible. If you have no use for the wood, then return it to Nature. Pile it into an unused corner or hedgerow and let the insect world reclaim it.

The wood from the smaller branches is very interesting as it has soft pith running through the centre. This can be poked out, leaving you with a hollow tube. These can be used for panpipes and whistles and for blowing the fire. They also make wonderful natural beads. Cut them to size with a small saw, take off the bark and sand them up, beginning with rough sandpaper, then medium and finishing with fine.

Herbal and Edible Uses: *Sambucus nigra*

Warning: Be clear that you are using the European Elder, as the fresh parts of the American Elder (*Sambucus canadensis*) can be poisonous.

This beautiful tree has been used medicinally for thousands of years and was known as the 'medicine chest of the country people'.

The Flowers

The mass of fragrant white Elderflowers is the signal that Summer has arrived. Harvest the first flowers in May and June, dry them in brown paper bags and store them in dark glass jars. (Sunlight will damage their properties.) They make a refreshing herbal tea, which will act as a daily tonic. You can also drink an infusion (see page 35) before going to bed to promote peaceful sleep. Elderflowers can be made into a cordial, a champagne or wine. The fresh flowers can be sprinkled on the top of leafy salads and fruit salads, and added to sorbets, cheesecakes and pancakes. The whole flowerhead can be dipped in batter and deep-fried – delicious with cream and honey! (Do not wash the flowers, as this will destroy much of their fragrance.)

Medicinally, a hot infusion of the flowers is useful to promote perspiration in fevers (combine with Yarrow and Peppermint) and for clearing excess mucus from the head or lungs. It is also useful for hayfever, sinusitis and catarrh. Elderflowers are a diuretic and aid the action of the kidneys by eliminating toxins from the body. A cool infusion can be used for cuts, wounds, bruises and burns, for bathing inflamed and sore eyes, as an after-sun lotion, for sprains, swollen joints and as a general skin tonic. Apply to the temples to ward off headaches and to bring clarity to the mind.

The Leaves

The leaves can be picked fresh, warmed and applied to the temples to relieve nervous headaches. The bruised leaves will act as an insect repellent or you can make a strong infusion to use as a lotion to keep away midges and mosquitoes. It will last a day or two if kept cool.

The Root and the Bark

These make a black dye and are both strong laxatives that should not be used casually.

The Berries

Elderberries are rich in vitamins A and C and can be made into jam, wine and cordials. Drink hot with added cinnamon and ginger to relieve colds and coughs.

Healing Properties

Elder is useful for the relief of 'stuck' emotionally congested states. It will bring clarity, easing worries and night fears. It enables us to move more positively into cycles of transition and to move from endings into new beginnings. As old things finish, new possibilities always present themselves, but sometimes we need to energetically clear out the old before this can happen. We must prepare for change by releasing the hold the past may have on us. We have to let go of old outworn attitudes or habits that no longer serve us before we are free to welcome new possibilities.

Ceremony and ritual are useful tools for setting change in motion. This simple ceremony is very empowering and releasing. Light a candle, and as you do, make a pledge or commitment to something you know you want to change in your life:

'I pledge to leave behind...'

Light another candle for what you welcome into your life:

'I welcome...'

Spirit
of the
Land

Scattered across the world are the sacred sites of our ancestors, who lived close to the land and had a deep connection to the Earth and its living energy. Their world was not confined to the world of surface reality, but embraced the world of Spirit – Spirit in the land, Spirit in the rocks, the Waters, the trees, the plants, the animals and the birds. Spirit was in all of life, whether it visibly breathed or not. Life was seen to be cyclical. As our ancestors followed the changing cycles of the Earth, the Sun and the Moon, they understood that endings created new beginnings, that rebirth followed death. Their spirituality grew from their own experiences.

Social memory was maintained mainly by oral tradition through story, song and place. Many of the stories have survived as our myths and legends, handed down through generations, providing an encoded symbolism and a link with our past.

Our Celtic ancestors acknowledged and explored their inner world, which was completely and inherently linked to their outer world. They accessed it by consciously journeying into the Otherworld or Dreamtime, following Spirit paths in the mind and on the land. They created sacred places in the landscape where land and stones enhanced these abilities.

Even now we find ourselves drawn towards the sacred sites of our ancestors. Their power and presence are still tangible today. Here we catch a glimpse of another reality within ourselves, experiencing a shift in perception and a deeper connection to the Spirit of the land.

We all have a natural ability to sense a different 'atmosphere', but we do not always fully trust these perceptions, often blocking them or ignoring them as fast as we receive them. We have been discouraged from believing that these senses are reliable and trustworthy and yet we all have experiences that fall outside the accepted conventions of normality, such as coincidences, synchronicity, telepathy, clairvoyance, déjà vu and intuitive communication with people and animals.

We can consciously explore these abilities by connecting to our inner stillness and developing our 'inner listening' skills. To do this we must be 'centred' and 'grounded' so that we are stable and in control.

Grounding

'Grounding' or 'earthing' ourselves is a useful technique to practise before and after any deep inner work or if we feel fearful, rushed or nervous, are in a big crowd or feel out of control at any time.

The simplest way to ground yourself is to breathe slowly and deeply and let your energy drop down to your lower belly and then down into the Earth. Grounding also stops us from becoming depleted. We tap into the unlimited source of energy in the Earth and power flows through us, not out of us, as we draw from the calm vitality of the Earth.

Some Grounding Exercises

🌲 Always begin by connecting to your breath. Breathe in deeply, right into your belly, and empty all the Air from your lungs as you breathe out. Breathe slowly and calmly. As you breathe in, feel the Air revitalizing and energizing you. As you breathe out, see anything you need to let go of dissolving into the Earth.

When you become practised at this, you might like to try one of the following.

🌲 Visualize yourself as a tree, with your body as the trunk, your arms as the branches and your feet extending into roots growing down into the Earth. Visualize your roots branching out into the dark fertile soil, growing around rocks and anchoring you to the Earth, as you draw in her goodness, stability and strength.

🌲 Stand with your legs a little apart and your feet firmly on the ground.

Place your open hands on your thighs, with your fingers spread, and picture your energy travelling down your legs into the Earth.

🌲 Breathe deeply and slowly and make a sighing 'Haaaaaaaaaaah' with each exhalation. Let energy flow through you to deep in the ground, where it will be cleansed and renewed. With each in-breath picture the energy from the Earth being drawn up into your lungs and filling your body with vitality and strength. This is a circular motion which brings connection and renewal.

Spirit of Place and Earth Energy

We all respond to the atmospheres of different places, finding some places welcoming, some friendly or healing and some sad, frightening or disturbing. This is not always a conscious response and is sometimes subjective, depending on our own state of mind at the time. Sometimes though, the same impressions or visions are sensed by lots of people independently, which suggests that a place is able to hold a memory, perhaps of events that happened there in the past, that can be tapped into.

It takes a special kind of inner stillness and courage to be able to enter a place that has a different feel, especially if you are not completely comfortable with it. Only open yourself if you feel completely safe. If in doubt, don't! Stay grounded and visualize a spiral of white light around you, keeping you safe. If you are emotionally low or unstable, do not go to such places unless they are known for their healing energies, or you feel the energy there is very healing for you. Always follow your own feelings and don't ignore the signs! Signs are synchronistic or coincidental things that happen at significant moments and can be interpreted as messages from the Spirit world.

Use a detailed map to explore your locality, paying special attention to any old wells or springs, cairns, burial mounds, tumuli, standing stones, ancient woodland, old churches, hilltops, caves, hidden valleys and ancient trackways or old green roads. These may prove to be special places of Earth energy, places where you may experience a reality shift, slipping out of time into a daydream or Dreamtime.

Experiment with ways of connecting to the natural energy of the land. You can do this by creating mental and symbolic links to whatever you wish to explore. This can be aided by humming instinctively and slipping into a chant you can repeat over and over again as new words and new insights come to you. Sing and speak to the Spirit of the land, the trees, the river, the animals and the birds. This is how you introduce yourself and tune in to the Spirit of the place, taking all the time in the world and slipping out of time in the process.

Communication outside our normal reality takes a bit of practice, but seems to be a very natural thing to do. If you watch young children play or remember how you played as a child, the distinction between the imagined world and normal reality is blurred. This suggests a natural ability that we all are born with but have lost touch with, encouraged by our society to stay firmly in the 'real world'. The first step to regaining this lost art is to acknowledge that our perceptions and intuitions can be trusted and that we need not fear them.

Dowsing or Divining with Rods or Pendulum

Dowsing is a practical way of gaining access to our intuition. It is a natural ability and we can all learn to do it. It can be used for establishing a course of action and for any enquiry where the answer is hidden. Dowsing or divining can also be used to find paths of Earth energy, underground Water or underground metals and helps us to track what is invisible to the naked eye.

Dowsing tools are varied, but include a pendulum, metal divining rods or L-rods and a fresh forked stick, especially from the Hazel tree. Dowsing can be done directly over the land or over a map.

Modern scientists call dowsing the 'bio-resonance method' and it has been used by oil and Water companies the world over to find supplies or detect problems underground. The police sometimes use a professional dowser to find things that have been hidden or buried. The practice has become accepted by the modern world because of its high success rate, although it is a seemingly illogical and ancient art.

Learning to Dowse

All dowsing tools work in the same way, essentially a binary readout of 'yes' or 'no'. Establish the signal for 'yes' by asking a question that you already know the answer to and observing the response of your dowsing tool. Usually a pendulum will move in a circle or swing backwards and forwards and the L-rods will cross over. Once you have established the response for 'yes', then keep this fixed from this moment onwards.

Ask questions that lead to a 'yes' or 'no' answer. The answer is in the question and in asking the right question. At the centre of the process is our ability to hold the intent, question or quest clearly in our mind. This is at the heart of all the skills that allow us conscious access to our unconscious minds.

Geomancy

Geomancy is the art of tuning in to the Earth by dowsing or divining the underground paths of energy, underground Water currents, mineral veins, metals, geological faults or streams of electromagnetic energy. These can all be detected using a pendulum, dowsing rods or a forked stick.

Sometimes the Earth's energy can become disturbed, blocked or stagnant, creating harmful geopathic Earth energies known to dowsers as 'black water'. These emit unhealthy vertical emissions which have an adverse effect on those who live above them. They cause a pronounced drop in well-being, lack of concentration and lack of energy, especially when people sleep directly over them. In extreme cases, this can develop into nervous system disorders and cancer. A professional dowser can be called in and will know how to redirect the harmful energy around the house using copper pipes or needles (see Networking Solutions).

Ley Lines, Spirit Paths and Dragon Paths

These are invisible pathways on the land along which energy can travel.

They connect the sacred sites of our ancestors, linking places of powerful Earth energy together. Though they cannot be seen, they can be sensed as well as dowsed. They pass through old hillforts, stone circles, barrows, tumuli, burial mounds and old churches (which were often built on the sacred sites of the past). It is a vast network of interlinking energy.

This system has been likened to the meridian system of the body, which links acupoints together. These channels and points are invisible to our eyes but exist as surely and definably as the nerves and can be understood as pathways of magnetic energy in the body. An acupuncturist or shiatsu practitioner keeps this energy flowing by applying acupuncture needles, pressure or heat to these points, restoring good health and equilibrium to the body.

Sacred sites can be seen as the acupoints of the land, with the stones activating the energy. The ancient custom of lighting beacon fires on the hilltops at each of the old seasonal festivals may be the same as the acupuncturist applying heat to activate and clear energies in the body.

Ley lines are also known as Spirit paths, along which Spirit travels. They link the ancient sites together and it may be that in the past they were used to link groups of people in different parts of the country who were initiated into out-of-body practices. In the past it was understood that a house should never be built on these paths and they should never be obstructed in any way or bad luck would follow.

These paths were also called dragon paths or faerie paths. The slaying of the dragon may have been an ancient system of geomancy where dragon paths were 'staked' to release any blockages in the Earth's energy system.

Stone Circles and Standing Stones

Many of the ancient sacred sites have been lost or converted to Christian sites, but an astounding amount still remain, considering that most were built between 5000 and 500 BC. They are concentrated along the Western side of Britain, from Cornwall to the farthest isles of Northern Scotland. They are found in Wales, all over Ireland, especially in the Southwest, all along the Atlantic coast of Europe through France, Portugal and Spain, and in Germany.

Many of the stone circles show unusual magnetic anomalies. In Britain, 80 percent of them are built either on or within a mile of a geological faultline. Paul Devereux's research projects have shown that out of the 286 stone circles in Britain today, 235 of them are found on Pre-Armorican rock outcrops. These are more than 250 million years old and cover only 36 percent of the landmass of Britain. This old crystalline granite stone is a mixture of different types of quartz, which could be acting as a condenser, storing electric charge until something triggers a discharge, such as the dawn light hitting the stones.

The Dragon Project recorded various anomalies at the Rollright stone circle in Oxfordshire, amongst other ancient sites in Britain. Using ultrasonic detectors and Geiger counters, the research team recorded abnormal pulses from the land around the stone circle which fluctuated dramatically according to the cycles of the Solstices and Equinoxes. Their most astounding discovery occurred inside the circle at dawn on the Winter Solstice. When the team stepped inside the circle with their detectors, the normal background level of ultrasound which their instruments were picking up ceased. There was silence within the circle! Interestingly, they detected an *increase* in ultrasonic readings within the circle at the Equinoxes!

The findings of the Dragon Project suggest that the Neolithic people chose very specific sites for their stone circles — places that created unusually high magnetic fields and static electric, ultrasonic and infrared discharges, especially at dawn. We know that our ancestors gathered at the stone circles at dawn at the Equinoxes and Solstices to watch the sunrise. As we are electromagnetic beings, it could be that they were there to do more than just watch the sunrise — they were there to interact with the electrical energy of the stones and the land.

The Rollright stones, Oxfordshire

Burial Mounds, Dolmens and Barrows

These are man-made mounds from the Neolithic and Bronze Ages, dating from 4000 BC to 700 BC. Barrows all over the world were constructed in similar ways, consisting of large stones creating a stone chamber. Some had a passageway of large flat stones leading into a central chamber. The whole structure was covered with Earth. But this was not just thrown over the top. It was made of layers of different clays and stones and sometimes faced with quartz chips. Sometimes the clay was not local, which again points to the very specific use of materials. These layers of organic and non-organic materials seem to shield the inside of the chamber from geomagnetic fields. It has been found that these sites emit an increase in radioactivity.

The stillness and power of these burial mounds are still tangible when you go into them and it is now thought that they may not have been places where the dead were buried but places where people went to communicate with the ancestors and enter the Otherworld or Dreamtime.

These are the entrances to the Otherworld we are told about in folktales — the 'faerie hills', 'dragon hills' and 'hollow hills', entrances to the kingdom of Faerie or to the dragon hoards, places where 'treasure' was to be found and time ran differently.

They are good places for meditation, chanting and sound healing. They create conditions that are conducive to telepathy, clairvoyance, receptivity to psychic activity and inner journeying. Inner journeying is a technique that has survived from many shamanic traditions and involves consciously travelling from this reality to other parts of our psyche.

Fogous

A fogou is a Cornish subterranean tunnel and chamber, built around 5000 BC. The chamber is a beehive structure with the passage leading into it. Fogous may have been used for initiation rites, as they resemble a birth canal and an Earth womb. They may also have been used for the practice of 'incubation', which goes back to Mesopotamia and the dawn of civilization. In ancient Egypt, it was known as 'temple sleep' and involved incubating dreams at specific sacred sites. Ancient China had special temples for incubatory rituals and dreaming and used them as an aid to political decision making.

In ancient Greece, temple sleep was used mainly to find cures for illnesses. The person seeking healing would go into a dream temple to sleep on a special bed. Temple assistants known as therapeutes would interpret their dreams, advising them on a course of treatment indicated by the contents of the dream.

Natural Caves

Natural caves provide us with the opportunity to go inside the Earth for contemplation, meditation, chanting, sound healing and inner journeying. They bring us closer to the Earth by being inside her and they can bring us closer to crystal outcrops or underground Water as well.

Natural caves can be seen as natural Earth wombs. They give us an experience of dark and silence. In the past they may have been used for healing and initiation. Narrow passageways were used as 'birth canals' for rites of passage involving rebirth into a new life or calling.

Springs and Wells

The sites of springs and old wells are usually places of special atmosphere. They are an interface between the elements of Earth and Water. The Water that comes out of the land has sometimes been inside the Earth for hundreds of years and travelled for thousands of miles, pouring over rock and crystal, seeping through porous rock, through underground fissures, dissolving rock and minerals. It has been purified and energized by the Earth before it reaches the surface.

Drinking pure spring water directly out of the Earth is a luxury to us today, but in the past it was our ancestors' lifeline and springs and wells were honoured by decorating them with flowers in the Spring and early Summer. Many of the old springs have now been forgotten, but some can be found and honoured once again.

If you are drawn to a site of an old spring or well, let its own special Spirit or energy guide you. You may feel you want to become a human guardian of the place, making sure its special energy is honoured and protected. There will also be ancient Spirit guardians protecting the spring and you will need to honour these energies as well as the living Waters that come from the Earth's womb. Offer a gift to the Spirit of the Waters and the guardians of the spring. This could be any special thing from Nature – a painted stone or something that has been made in a sacred way using natural materials such as clay or wood. These are known as votive offerings and may be placed nearby or dropped into the Water itself. Ribbons or prayer flags may be hung from a nearby tree.

Sacred Gardening

Experience a different approach to gardening by exploring the Earth energies in your garden! This involves working with the natural energies in intuitive and creative ways and not imposing your will on Nature. Choose plants for their inherent energy and herbal properties rather than for the way they look. Spend time tuning in to the special energy or 'feel' of the plants and sensing any impressions you receive.

Experiment with dowsing for the geopathic energies that may be in your garden. Begin by establishing your intention firmly in your mind and your wish to use the signal for 'yes' to indicate where they are. See if any run through your house. If you find they run through where you usually sit or lie in bed, then move the furniture off the line and call in a professional dowser to redirect them around the house (*see Networking Solutions*).

Although not good for us, geopathic energies have been found to improve the production of compost bins or compost toilets when they are placed over them, as they stimulate certain microbes and insects. Bees, too, seem to enjoy these geopathic energies, speeding up honey production in hives placed over them. Both cats and ants are drawn to these places of geopathic energy.

If you intuitively sense any areas of stagnant energy in the garden, then bury, place or half-bury a piece of granite, quartz or crystal there. This will help to release and revitalize the energy of the Earth and the immediate surroundings.

Create a place in your garden for quiet contemplation, a sheltered place to sit by night or day. Choose plants for their healing qualities and what you wish to bring to the area. Include the Five Elements – a stone or tree for Earth, a pond or fountain for Water, wind chimes or a bird table for Air, a fire pit or somewhere for candle lanterns to hang for Fire and a central shrine stone for Spirit. This central stone is a wonderful contemplation table on which you can put seasonal things and charge up plant essences in the sunlight and crystals in the moonlight.

No matter how small your garden, let a bit of wilderness in – even if it is a dark North-facing spot you can do little else with! Include native woodland plants that grow well in shade. Put a log and some stones there and then leave them for insects, spiders and small animals to live in and for native plants to reclaim. If you have a larger garden, create a wildlife corner by planting native flowers and trees and leaving it undisturbed.

Vision Quest

A vision quest is a journey into the land to seek vision and understanding. It is time out from your everyday life and you go alone. It may last for a day or several days, sleeping out on the Earth. Choose an area that has some ancient connections or an area you are drawn towards.

Usually you eat only fruit and nuts and drink only spring water during a vision quest. You step out with awareness, making your sacred connection to the land with each step and each breath. You follow your intuition and have no plans – you let Spirit guide you. That is not to say you have no choice. Every step of the way you have choice. It is the intuitive faculties you use for making those choices that are different from usual and that put you in a different space from usual.

You may have a specific question you are asking for help with. You may wish to spend much of the day in meditation or go on an inner journey with your question or intention held clearly in your mind. You may not have a specific question but decide to be open to the wisdom of the Earth and the vision quest experience.

A vision quest is different from just a day out. You are absorbed in your quest, your focus. It becomes your walking meditation. You notice any signs or omens from the land — sky, clouds, birds, insects or animals. You find inner stillness and largely stay silent unless for necessary communication or if you feel moved to make sounds, sing or chant or speak out loud to Spirit.

You emerge from your vision quest with an experience of the interconnectedness of all things, in touch with your inner knowing and the wisdom of the Earth and with an answer to your questions and a vision for your future direction.

Rowan

Sorbus aucuparia

'Tree of inner vitality, intuition and protection'

The beautiful Rowan is known as 'the Lady of the Mountains' or Mountain Ash and grows higher up the sides of mountains than any other native tree. It does not grow very tall, so plant this delightful little tree in your garden and bring its clear mountain energy into your life.

It is the 2nd tree in the Celtic Tree Ogham, representing inner vitality, spiritual strength, increased psychic abilities, intuition and protection.

The planetary ruler of Rowan is Mercury. In mythology, the winged god Mercury is also linked to serpent energy and carries the caduceus, the double snaked symbol of healing.

The Rowan tree is a delight to look at in all seasons, with its profusion of white flowers in the Spring, bright red berries in the early Autumn and vibrant red and orange leaves in late Autumn. The bright clusters of Autumn berries bring the birds into your garden, especially blackbirds and thrushes, as they love to eat them. This helps to grow new trees as the birds disperse the seeds around the garden and the surrounding countryside.

Growing Rowan Trees

If you find you have some of these self-seeded Rowan trees in your garden, then dig them up in the Autumn or Winter and move them to sites where they can mature. You can mark them with a piece of coloured wool in the early Autumn so that you can find them once their leaves have dropped.

To grow Rowan trees, collect the ripe seeds in the Autumn, wash the flesh from them and stratify them in the following way.

Stratification

Most tree seeds need exposure to the cold of at least one Winter, sometimes two. The technique of stratification mimics the natural process of Nature. In cool Autumns, germination can be improved by keeping stratifying seeds at room temperature for two weeks before putting them outside for the Winter.

- Mix the washed seeds with an equal amount of stratification mixture. This is peat-free potting compost mixed with an equal amount of a coarse particle material such as bark chips, perlite, sand or grit.
- Put the seeds and growing mixture into large pots with good drainage, cover with mesh or wire to keep out rodents and either bury in the ground, place against a North-facing wall or keep in a cool outhouse. It is important that the mixture remains moist but not saturated.
- In the Spring tip out the mixture and remove any seeds that are beginning to germinate. These can be planted in large individual pots. Put any seeds that haven't germinated back into the mixture and check it every week during the Spring. It is important to sow the new shoots

immediately, as they get damaged more easily if they get too large.

If any seeds are not germinating, it is possible that they need two Winters before germination.

Folklore and Legend

Rowan has always been known as a tree of protection. It was planted next to the house to prevent evil spirits from entering and used as protection against enchantments and illness. Rowan twigs were hung over the door, strewn across the path, hung on the beam of the fireplace, tied onto the bedhead or poked into a keyhole. The young twigs were woven into collars to protect Spring lambs and hung from the brow bands of ponies and horses.

From earliest times Rowan trees were associated with sacred sites and legend has it that they were guarded by a dragon or serpent. This has obvious links to the dragon hills and the dragon paths of Earth energy; perhaps the Rowans marked and guarded the dragon or dragon paths. Rowans were traditionally planted in graveyards in Wales to protect the dead. As many of the early churches were built on the old sacred sites, the Rowans could have been there already and the custom continued.

Rowan is associated with an increase in psychic abilities and divination, particularly increased ability to receive forewarnings or knowledge of previously unknown outside influences.

Rowan trees were used as assembly points before going into battle, possibly due to their significant locations on the old sacred sites. Rowan sticks were burnt before battles to seek out any omens, signs or direction from the Spirit realms. Rowan has long been linked to runes and charms, especially those involving protection and divination.

A forked Rowan twig was used to divine the presence of underground metals.

The Wisdom of Rowan

Rowan or Mountain Ash is a tree of great vitality, able to grow high in the mountains and often found growing out of tight crevices, clinging on to life despite its difficult situation. This teaches us to make the most of life, to hold on to our own path and to follow what is right and life-affirming.

Rowan is also called the Quickening tree. It brings a quickening of energy on all levels, an awareness of life's pulse and interconnectedness with other levels of existence. Rowan helps us to work with energy, to tune in to the Spirit of place and to the trees, to develop our creative powers and impulses, our intuitive responses and psychic abilities.

Rowan teaches us to be open to all possibilities, bringing a quickening of creativity. If we act on these impulses we are giving life to our deepest wishes. Each Rowanberry has a five-pointed star or pentacle at its base. This ancient symbol of protection represents the Five Elements that make up all of life: Earth, Air, Fire, Water and Spirit, with Spirit as the point at the top.

The Wood and Its Uses

Rowan wood was once popular for tool handles, including the handles of ceremonial tools. It is a lovely wood to carve.

Rowan makes an excellent walking stick, bringing an increase in psychic abilities and intuition. This makes it especially good for night walking. Rowan can also be used for making divination tools such as runes or Ogham sticks (see page 40).

Making a Healing Wand or Touchwood

A healing wand can be used intuitively to enhance any healing technique. The essential healing qualities of the tree are accessed through contact with the wood and with the Spirit of the tree and are directed through use of the wand.

A touchwood is a smooth piece of wood you carry in your pocket or wear around your neck, again accessing the healing qualities of the tree through touch.

If you wish to make a healing wand from Rowan, spend time with the tree first and ask for its blessing. Be guided by your intuition and, with heartfelt thanks, cut the twig you are drawn towards.

When you first cut your wand, meditate with it, work with its essential energy and let the Rowan guide you. Picture the tree and its location in your meditations and in your healing work, creating links to the tree from which the wand came.

Use sandpaper to make yourself a smooth touchwood. Work through the different grades of sandpaper until you are using the finest grade available. This brings out a skin-soft smoothness that is a joy to touch.

Rather than discarding the fine twigs you have left over, put them into a vase of Water to honour and celebrate the tree from which they came.

Herbal and Edible Uses: *Sorbus aucuparia*

The Berries

Harvest the berries in September and dry them in brown paper bags or on paper sheets out of direct sunlight. When they are completely dry, store them in dark glass jars or brown paper bags. When you need them, make a decoction (see page 35) by soaking them overnight in cold Water. They are a good source of vitamin C and the juice is an antiseptic. It can be used as a mild laxative and as a gargle for sore throats and hoarseness.

Use the fresh berries for Rowanberry wine and Rowanberry jelly. Cooked with other fruit, they can be made into pies or fruit pudding.

Healing Properties

Rowan has an airy wisdom and strengthens our positive life energy and our personal power, bringing healing to the Spirit.

It also brings a connection to the kundalini or serpent force, which is the vital life force in the body. It travels up from the base of the spine to the crown, the seat of our spiritual connection. Rowan is linked to fertility and the new life that the rising tide of fertile energy brings.

Spend time with Rowan trees whenever you need their uplifting energy. They bring the bright clarity of the mountains into your thoughts and encourage far-sighted visions and insights.

Spirit of
Rowan

Creating Change

We are all capable of changing ourselves, our situation, our circumstances, the way we think and the way we live our lives. We are free to grow, to flow, to discover, to know when something feels right and good and to act upon it. We can initiate change through various techniques that help the process along and through our determination to follow the path of the heart. This leads to natural caring and goodwill, which become anchored in our daily lives and affect all our choices and decisions. This is where the real change lies. Everything else follows from here.

Change does not have to happen all at once but can become part of an ongoing process. We integrate what we have learned from our experiences and they become part of who we are and the direction we are heading in.

Mutual loving relationships

Daily Practice

Every day put aside 10 minutes or more to connect consciously to your heart and the changes you wish to bring into your life. Daily practice helps to bring focus and, by its repetition, helps to remind you of your new intentions. Choose from the following, keeping one focus for at least a month:

✒ Begin the day by stretching and a few gentle exercises. This energizes the body and releases energy so that it can flow freely. It is especially important to keep your joints open and free and to be aware of any areas where energy feels blocked or stiff. Do be gentle with yourself and do not do anything which causes you pain. If there are any areas where the build-up has already taken hold, keep the energy physically moving as well as visualizing the flow and movement becoming easier. Look for areas of your life that are aggravating the condition and find ways of changing them.

✒ Begin the day by facing the East, the place of the rising Sun. Welcome the opportunity for new beginnings that each new day brings. This simple act can transform your relationship to all you do.

✒ Before you rise, give thanks for the many things in your life that you feel grateful for and take a few minutes to think about all the people you Love, sending them good wishes for the day.

✒ If you are aware of a negative affirmation you often make to yourself, then create a new positive statement to replace it and say it over and over again to yourself during the day until you feel that it is creating changes in your life. For example, if you feel that you are always rushed and haven't enough time, affirm to yourself that you have plenty of time for all you want to do. It's surprising what a huge difference this makes to your day. Everything flows more easily when you do not feel rushed and time actually 'stretches'.

🖋 Make one morning pledge for each day, one thing you will do for yourself, one thing that feeds your soul. Choose something that you know is possible. Each small achievement adds to the greater whole.

🖋 If you wish to make changes in your life, repeat each day what you wish for. Speak in the present tense, as if the change is already upon you, and hold a strong image in your mind's eye that what you wish for is already on its way to you. You can also buy a special candle for this, lighting it each time you make your affirmation and placing anything beside it that helps you to see your new way forward.

🖋 Keep a morning journal for a while. Write down any dreams or insights you may have had on waking. Share 15 minutes with yourself when you first wake up, writing down anything that comes to you, without thinking about it, editing it or planning it. This is a fantastic way to connect to your deeper levels. If possible, do this every day for two months.

🖋 Once in a while, detox for the day, drinking only spring water and eating only organic fruit. Eat and drink with awareness and gratitude for the gifts of the Earth and your body.

🖋 At the end of the day, before you go to sleep, face the West and thank the day for what it has brought you, focusing on what you are grateful for. A daily review before you go to sleep helps you remember your day and brings continuity into your life. Working backwards, take each thing you did frame by frame. Do not judge yourself or get caught up in any of the problems. Do your best to bring a loving energy to your review, sending Love to those who need it, including yourself. If you *do* have any problems, look for a loving response you could make and be open to solutions from remembered dreams.

Meditation

Meditation is a must for anyone who wishes to create change in their lives, as it creates change from within. It is well documented that meditation brings peace of mind, reduces stress, helps with problem solving and increases our ability to concentrate and stay focused. It is a way of stilling the mind and finding peace within.

How to Meditate

There are many different ways to meditate, but they all employ the same technique. This is basically to concentrate the mind on one single point in order to slip beyond it to a place of no mind, no thought, no time and 'nothingness'. We can meditate on many different things: on our breath, a symbol, a feeling, an image, a colour, a flower, a candle flame, the Five Elements, a tree or a picture. The choice is ours. It depends on what works for us and what we need at the time.

Once we are practised at finding our connection to the still place within, we can link to it instantly whenever we need it: we can simply put ourselves there and we are there.

First, though, we have to find this place and practise the art of effortlessly 'being'.

1. Begin by sitting comfortably, straight-backed if possible. Crossed-legged is good if that is comfortable. Lean against a wall or a tree or sit on a cushion or meditation stool.

2. Close your eyes, take some deep breaths and take a few minutes to settle your energy, letting it drop from your head into your belly.

3. Become aware of yourself as you sit — where you are, how you are feeling — and then gently begin to focus your thoughts on your breath.

4. Feel each breath as you breathe in and out through your nose. Keep your focus on your breath and your breath alone. Focus on the tip of your nose where the breath is entering and leaving your body.

5. Whenever you become aware that you are thinking, observe your thoughts briefly and then gently and firmly bring your concentration back to your breathing.

6. There will be times when all thoughts, including the awareness of the breath, have gone. This is an inner resting place, which replenishes us like a good night's sleep. It also clears the way for our intuition to come through more easily. It brings clarity and contentment, a feeling of well-being.

Put aside 10 minutes every day to still your mind in meditation and after a while you will find the benefits begin to show. Eventually, as you become practised at finding that still point within, you will find that those 10 minutes have extended and that your connection to the still place within is coming to you much more easily.

The Inner Smile Meditation

1. Begin in the usual way, breathing deeply as you connect to that still, centred feeling. Take your time over this until you feel at peace inside yourself.

2. Then picture in your mind someone or something that makes you happy, makes you smile.

3. Catch that inner smile, that feeling of happiness, and feel it as it washes through you. Feel the light of twinkling-smile-energy all around you. Bathe in its light, in the wonderful smile it brings to you, sending it to any parts of your body that need its healing energy.

4. After you have done this, send it out to anyone you know who may need it. Feel them receiving it as you picture it washing over them.

5. Send it out into the world, to specific countries, anywhere you want to send its goodness and light. Know that its energy is received on a subtle level, as all things are connected.

Earth Meditations

🌲 Make a commitment at least once every week to find some way to connect deeply to the Earth. Take a walk, go to the woods or a sacred site, climb a hill, sit with a tree, work in your garden, grow or gather some of your food, and do so in a meditative way. Lose the clamour of your thoughts as you commune with the Earth. Slip out of time into a daydream state. It's very good for you!

🌲 Find a place to sit with a tree or a group of trees, a place where you feel comfortable and welcomed. Breathing deeply and rhythmically, gently place every thought to one side as it comes into your mind until you can feel your connection to the land and the trees. Practise sitting as still as possible and observe the sounds, smells and colours and the comings and goings of wildlife. A group of people can sit in stillness in the same area and share their impressions afterwards.

🌲 Each day take a moment to feel yourself rooted to the Earth. This brings stability and stillness. It can be as simple as imagining your roots going down into the Earth. Feel your outbreath extending down into the Earth and feel your inbreath drawing up her vitality and goodness. This can be done anytime and anywhere without anyone noticing that you are doing it.

🌲 This can be extended if you have a little more time and can sit for five or ten minutes. Follow your roots down into the Earth, as they weave through the soil, around rocks, encountering other forms of life, bones or remains from the past. Keep going down until you reach the living core of fiery energy at the centre of the Earth. Draw this living energy up into your body, feeling its vitality becoming part of your energy. Finally, visualize a place on the Earth where you feel completely comfortable and rest a while, feeling held and nurtured by the Earth. Look upon it all as a little journey, a kind of waking dream, and see where it takes you.

🌲 Take a second or two before you eat to thank the Earth for your food. This is such a simple act and yet it will transform your whole relationship to food and to the Earth. Bless and give thanks for a glass of spring water and consciously take its pure life-giving goodness within. Gratitude and blessings are both acts of transformation that open our hearts and bring remarkable changes, healing, inner peace, good health and happiness.

Creating a Ceremony

Ceremony provides a framework that we can use to make connections to our feelings and our own personal spirituality. We can do this on our own or with friends to support and nourish each person's unique spiritual path and development. This creates lasting friendships and brings the bonding of community into our lives.

Ceremony does not have to come from any tradition, but we can bring new ideas to some traditional sacred acts such as blessings, prayer, dedication, anointing, blessing a baby, marriage and funerals. Grassroots spirituality is inventive and open. We are free to create our own ceremonies and to create sacred space wherever we feel it is appropriate. This might be outside or within our homes. We have no priest or priestess. We are all as important and powerful as each other. We help each other to stay in touch with our hearts, our feelings and our Love. We encourage each other to be beautiful and powerful. Power is not something to wield over others, but something to help us to believe in ourselves, to act from our feelings and to use to protect the Earth.

Ceremony can help us to release the past, let go of what has crushed us, put us down, controlled us, dampened our Spirit and made us feel weak, inadequate or fearful. Ceremony can help us to focus on what we know needs changing in our lives and find new ways forward.

We can use ceremony to mark and celebrate a new beginning, a new outlook and new directions in life. We can make and share personal pledges together. We can invite friends to witness and support us in a change we wish to announce or a rite of passage we wish to experience. Ceremony helps us to receive guidance from our natural inner wisdom. We can use ceremonial space to honour, to bless, to heal, to dedicate, to give thanks and to energize. A ceremony brings focus to the way forward and enables us to understand our own spiritual journey.

It does not matter that we do not stick to one formula – we can try out different ideas, see which feels right at the time, what we enjoy doing and what rings true. We can develop our own unique ways to connect to the sacred. It does not matter if our understanding of Spirit changes. That is the deepening of our experience and the developing of our spiritual path.

We can also gather with friends to participate in celebrating each of the eight Celtic festivals, renewing our connection to the Earth and the seasons. These fall every six weeks or so and are a wonderful opportunity to review the six weeks that have just gone by and decide on possible directions for the coming six weeks.

Intention

Take some quiet time to become clear about your intention before you begin any ceremonial, healing or energy work. Build up a picture of what it is you want to do. We all influence the energy fields around us, whether we are conscious of this or not. By choosing to influence them by our positive intent we set off a chain of events that improve our lives in many unforeseen ways. Energy radiates out from us with an inner vitality. Like always attracts like and we draw towards us that which our intention has set in motion.

Opening a Ceremony

It is both good and necessary to mark clearly the moment when ceremonial space is beginning. It puts us in the right frame of mind and helps us to focus on our intentions. It is always good to begin with a grounding exercise, breathing deeply, letting our energy drop from the head, down through the body and into the Earth (see page 87).

Creating sacred space can be as simple as taking a moment to stand in stillness with the clear intention of creating a change in focus. This is spirituality from the heart. It grows out of our own inner understanding, our own spiritual connections and our own imagination. There are no rules, only that we work for our greater good, for the greater good of all and the greater good of the Earth.

If we come together with other people, we can begin by holding hands in a circle and letting our collective meditation bring attunement and shared harmony as we create a sacred circle. We can begin with a chant or song, meditation, guided visualization, drumming or by sharing a common focus of healing or prayer. If you are very experienced at working together, let the whole thing flow spontaneously. Alternatively, decide on a framework at the beginning and then within this everyone is free to be spontaneous, saying and doing what comes from the heart.

A traditional way of beginning a ceremony is to acknowledge the Five Elements in turn, making a connection to each one in as heartfelt a way as possible and visualizing them forming a circle of energy around you.

The Centre of a Ceremony

It is better to keep a ceremony simple and heartfelt than to be too heady and complicated. Have one focus as the centre of the ceremony. This may include more than one activity, but hold the focus and explore the luxury of slowing down, with space for silence and contemplation.

The centre of a ceremony may be planned or spontaneous. It does require complete honesty and openness to our inner feelings, sense of goodness and intuition in order for it to work deeply. This is spirituality at its simplest and most accessible. No one is telling us how to do it and we can do whatever feels right.

Closing a Ceremony

Closing marks the end of the ceremony. If you acknowledged the Five Elements at the beginning, then acknowledge and thank them at the end. Explore ways that help you feel grounded and complete: maybe a reconnection to the grounding exercise you used at the beginning, a meditation, a chant or the sharing of bread with spring water or a fruit drink that has been blessed.

The Act of Transformation

When we come together in ceremonial circles we empower our lives. When we step back into our everyday lives we are in touch with ourselves in new ways. We have more confidence, a greater sense of our own worth, of who we are and where we are going.

We can also create ceremony and ritual on our own, taking the time out from our normal lives to create special moments of spiritual connection and renewal.

Ceremony is a form of alchemy. It brings change into our lives by transforming our heartfelt feelings and sense of rightness into positive action.

Alchemy is an act of transformation. The alchemists of old sought much more than the changing of base metal into gold. They were mystics, philosophers, psychologists, artists, poets and visionaries, men and women who were each following their own unique understanding of spirituality. They sought spiritual enlightenment, the transformation of the lowest, base parts of themselves in order to achieve the highest spiritual goals. They sought the meaning of life through their work with each of the Five Elements.

The Five Elements

Understanding the underlying energy of each of the Five Elements — Earth, Air, Fire, Water and Spirit — is the basis of any energy and healing work. These are the elements of life and they are honoured in all the spiritual traditions the world over. Each has a unique and special energy that we can learn to work with.

The meanings of each of the elements, even the names of the elements themselves, vary with different traditions around the world, but it is our connection to the underlying energy that matters, not their names.

The Celtic tradition is my starting point, but my relationship to the Five Elements and how to use them is an organic connection which is always developing. Nothing is fixed. I prefer to flow like the elements themselves, being guided by my deepening experience of their energy and how they interact.

The Wisdom of Earth

Earth represents the material world, the Earth herself and all that is manifest upon her. Mother Earth is the giver and provider of sustainable life. She nurtures and protects us, is supportive and nourishing.

The Earth's cycles keep us connected to the cycles of life through the seasonal flow. Each season is an opportunity for us to live our lives in harmony with the underlying energy of the Earth.

Earth is the fertile force, continuously creating life, abundant life. Death is rebirth in continuous cycles of life. We bury our dead within the Earth, knowing that it generates life from death. Earth is the regenerative force. Out of the darkness, death and decay of Winter comes the Spring, bringing new life, new growth.

We are physically anchored to the Earth. This brings stability and containment, firm foundations and deep-rooted connections. We can go inside the Earth, into caves and caverns, underground passages, burial mounds and tumuli. She helps us to appreciate the darkness, the stillness within her and within ourselves. Through this we experience our strong roots and deep connections. She gives us the Underworld, the world within, the Celtic Otherworld, the Aborigine Dreamtime, the Deep Mysteries, connection to our ancestors and our past.

We climb the Earth's mountains to gain peace and farsighted vision. We feel the pulse of her living rocks, crystals, minerals, standing stones and stone circles. We sense the ancient Earth dragons, the serpent force within the land, and we can sing with the ancient voices of the land, which brings us closer to our ancestors and their own understanding of the Earth.

We stand in awe of ancient trees, in forest and woodland, and know the deep friendship of the trees. We sense the presence of Nature spirits and the faerie realms. We gather fruit, herbs and vegetables to eat and store for the Winter, and know the joy of growing these ourselves. We grow flowers for pleasure and delight, to give as gifts, to mark a special occasion, for healing and to lift the Spirit.

Earth deserves our deepest gratitude, for all that we take, for our food and all the world's resources.

In the Celtic tradition, Earth is in the North and corresponds to the heart of Winter at the Winter Solstice. Here Earth teaches us the importance of the darkness where we can rest, finding regeneration and renewal from within. Earth represents growth, containment, nurturing, manifestation, stability and the world within.

The Wisdom of Air

Air is a connecting force as it circulates around the whole world. It touches us all on the inside as well as the out- side. My breath is your breath is our breath *ad infinitum*. Through our breath we are all connected — nations, friends and enemies alike — through all the generations and ages of life on Earth, going back into the mists of time.

Air speaks to us on the wind, from the subtle play of gentle breezes to the mighty hurricane, from freezing icy winds to warm balmy winds and hot desert winds.

Air can be electric or stagnant. It can hold a blueprint of energy and we can read its subtle changes whether they are caused by atmospheric weather conditions or by human emotions. We can sense when the air is charged positively or negatively, whether it is clear and bright or murky and dark. It affects us in unseen and subtle ways.

The winds of change blow through our lives. We cast caution to the wind and act on our instincts. The four winds bring the elemental angels, Spirit guides and messages from the Spirit world.

Air is the sky, the clouds, movement, travel, the realm of flight – flights of fancy, flights of inspiration, flights of the imagination, flights of the birds, butterflies, insects, faeries and dragons. Spirits of Air were called sylphs and were believed to be in communication with the Divine Source.

Air is the element of communication: words, poetry, song, sounds of all kinds from a whisper to a bellow. Our words have power and reveal our inner-most truths. Whispered words can send healing or harm. Our very breath moves energy. We can breathe out our pain and breathe in strength and courage. We blow out a birthday candle to send our wishes and hopes on their way.

Air is also the element through which our thoughts travel. We send out messages through our thoughts, whether these are conscious or not. We can also consciously direct our thoughts through focused intent. We can send healing, emotional signals, prayers, impressions. We can also receive these things. Telepathy and clairvoyance are deeper levels of this inherent ability.

Our thoughts can create harmony and lift the Spirits or can be destructive and even bring illness upon ourselves. Whatever we send out to others comes back to us. Air is always in motion and nothing in its nature is linear. Air swirls and eddies, whirls back on itself. It moves things along, whips things up and creates change. Meditation helps us to find peace and harmony within, stills our thoughts and rests our minds. It helps us to become aware of our thoughts and their influence on our lives and all we do.

Air is the Spirit of communication. Our world has become one global family through modern communication technology. We are no longer isolated: we are part of the 'We' of humanity. The nature of our communication with our global family is crucial to the healthy future of our planet. We are breaking free of the old patterns of competition, the need to win and be better than everyone else. We have to move beyond hate, violence, war, fear and need for revenge that has held the old worldview in its destructive little grasp. The more we engage in healthy, open, non-violent communication, sharing how we feel in as non-judgemental a way as possible, the more we are part of the new winds of change. The more we communicate from our hearts, the more others will feel inspired to do the same.

In the Celtic tradition, Air is in the East, at the dawn of a new day, the place of new beginnings. Air represents inspiration and visions. On the Wheel of the Year it is connected to the Spring Equinox, which is the point of perfect balance when day and night are equal in length. This place of balance brings union and harmony and is a fertile place for new growth and new life. Once we find this balance within ourselves we are able to direct our thoughts and intentions, sending Love's healing energy out into the world and into our lives.

The Wisdom of Fire

Fire is a catalyst, an element of change and transformation. It can save life and destroy life. It purifies, liberates and energizes. Out of the ashes the phoenix rises to bring a new beginning, new life from the destruction of the old.

Fire generates energy and is an active force – powerful, passionate and all-consuming. It will burn up, burn through and burn out. It smoulders and smokes, it glows, it sparks and flames, it roars and can become out of control as it burns everything in its path.

Fire is light that comes from the Sun and the stars, transferring energy from 'the above to the below'. Our eyes reflect our inner Fire. We shine our light from within and we kindle the sacred flame of our spirituality.

Fire is creative, the spark of life and the spark of inspiration. Fire is the life force, the serpent power. Fire dragons and the salamanders of myth and legend are not consumed by Fire and so represent original prime substance. Molten rock and Fire are at the heart of the Earth.

Fire symbolizes wild freedom, runaway energy. We burn with Love and with passion. We light the Fire of our sexuality.

The hearth Fire is at the heart of the home. We watch pictures form in the Fire, letting our imaginations loose, seeing visions and receiving impressions. We can burn away the past; burn away our limitations, burn off excess.

Fire is boldness and genius. Fire liberates action.

In Celtic tradition, Fire is in the South and connected to the high point of the solar cycle at the Summer Solstice. Its place is at midday, when the Sun is highest in the sky. Fire brings us expansive active power, courage and willpower, coupled with spontaneity and inspired action.

The Wisdom of Water

Our beautiful planet is full of Water. Water keeps everything in motion, replenished and cleansed. The oceans of our world keep us all connected. Water is the fertile force of life – Water of life, life-giving Water. In ancient legend Water is the creative force that brings forth life, healing, youthfulness and immortality. We all begin life swimming in the amniotic fluid of our mothers' wombs and our bodies are 75 percent water.

Water has many forms and many voices. It speaks to us from the mountain streams, the waterfalls, the rivers and the sea. We rest by rivers and lakes. We find stillness and fulfilment beside Water. Water can be life-giving, yet it can be destructive, as flood sweeps away everything in its path.

Water is a magical and mutable force which can dissolve rock and metal, turn solid into liquid and back again. It can become ice and create mighty tracts of land and it can evaporate into steam or condensation and be gone, only to reappear as Water again.

Water and the Moon are linked in an endless cycle of gravitational pull, creating the rhythmic swell and ebb of the oceans' tides. The Moon pulls on the Water in our bodies and can bring emotional instability, but this helps us to stay in touch with our feelings. Our watery nature helps our emotions to flow, keeping us healthy. It is important for our health that we express our emotions. Blocked emotional energy is often the root of ill health. We shed tears of sorrow, tears of laughter, tears of joy and tears of pain. Tears bring release. Don't hold back your tears!

Our watery emotions bring us deep insights into ourselves. When our cup flows over we feel blessed and abundant. We ride the crest of a wave when things are going well and we sink when things go badly. We throw coins into Water for good luck.

When we share our feelings with others we become closer and clearer in our friendships and understanding of each other. Water connects us to our deep unconscious selves, to Universal Love and the deep mystery of our soul purpose. Through Love and compassion we touch the depths of our souls.

Water is never still; it is always seeking its own level. It flows, swirls, gathers momentum, spirals, eddies and always takes the path of least resistance. If it becomes blocked, it builds up until it bursts the confines of the blockage, generating new energy from the Waters held back.

In the past wells were revered as Water passages to the womb of the Earth. They were of prime importance to any house, community or village and were blessed and dressed with flowers in the Spring to give thanks to the life-giving Waters. Offerings were made to the Spirits of Water, the Water sprites and the undines, to ensure good luck, good health and protection.

Water has a memory and is alive. It will hold an imprint sent from our thoughts. We can bless water, consecrate Water and change its molecular structure by our thoughts and prayers. Water can be used for cleansing, purifying, renewing, refreshing and revitalizing. It can be used for baptism, as a symbolic act of renewal and rebirth, to wash away and release the past, to dissolve past hurts and old rigid patterns, to help us let go of our deepest fears, to banish negativity and to consecrate.

Try not to drink the Water from our taps. It has no vitality left in it and contains harmful chemicals that could have an adverse affect upon us. Drink at least one glass of spring water before and after any healing work to help conduct the healing energy around the body. Drink plenty of spring Water when you are not well, if you are studying and during any mental or physical work.

In the Celtic tradition, Water is in the West, the place of the setting Sun and the beginning of night. On the Wheel of the Year, Water is at the Autumn Equinox. Here we turn within to nurture our inner selves and plant our personal seeds for the future. Water represents the heart, receptivity, the unconscious, flow, our emotions and cleansing.

The Wisdom of Spirit

Spirit is the Fifth Element, the Infinite Source and Essence of life. There is nothing in the universe that is not Spirit. It is the Infinite One, Omnipresent, Omnipotent, Unconditional Love, God, Goddess, Great Spirit, Infinite Energy, Infinite Love, the Eternal Timeless Truth, the Divine, Everlasting Source of All That Is.

All is vibration. All is in movement. Nothing rests. Everything vibrates with Spirit. We are all Spirit. We are all part of everything, always. Everything lives in Spirit and Spirit lives in everything. Spirit is the Limitless Is.

In the Celtic tradition, Spirit is the circle that has no beginning and no end. It is the centre and also the circumference. It is the connecting force. Through Spirit we are eternally part of all life and all that exists in all the worlds.

Hazel

Corylus avellana

'Tree of creative
change
and inspiration'

Hazel is a very distinctive tree seen in hedgerows and in woods. It has many straight stems or 'rods' growing from its base or 'stool' and has been long been coppiced (regularly cut back to ground level) to encourage more of these straight rods to grow. The Hazel's bright yellow catkins, seen in January and February, are one of the first signs that the Earth is awakening after her Winter sleep. This is a good time to note where Hazel trees are growing, as they stand out against a bare landscape.

Hazel is the 9th tree in the Celtic Tree Ogham and corresponds to nine, the number of wisdom and deep knowledge. It represents pure distilled knowledge, creative use of the intuition and inspired solutions.

Ruled by Mercury, Hazel has a quick-moving energy that will help us keep inspiration flowing and will amplify our connection to our intuition. It is associated with Brigid, the maiden goddess of hearth and home.

Hazel is a useful tree to grow in the garden and with regular coppicing will give a good supply of rods. These can be used to make archways, bowers, screens, windbreaks, plastic-covered greenhouses, garden sheds and other structures and will provide a good supply of pea and bean sticks.

Coppiced Hazel woodland is rich in wildlife, as regular cutting allows light to reach the woodland floor, benefiting the wild flowers and butterflies. Dormice and squirrels feed on the hazelnuts that ripen in September, so if you want to gather the nuts, pick them a little early when they are still green.

Growing Hazel Trees

Growing Hazel trees is very easy. Simply plant the nuts directly into a pot and leave them out to germinate over the Winter. It is a good idea to tie some netting over the pot to stop mice from digging the nuts up. In the Spring, the shell splits and out comes the root and then the shoot. Plant the young trees out in the Autumn after the leaves have fallen or transplant them into a bigger pot to plant out in the following Autumn.

Folklore and Legend

In Celtic legend, nine nuts of wisdom fell from the Hazel tree into the river. They were eaten by a magical salmon, which absorbed all the wisdom they contained. There are many workings of this same tale: the salmon changes into a young girl or the salmon is Fintan the White Ancient, who was able to take the form of animals, or the nuts fell into the Well of Life, causing bubbles of inspiration to rise to the surface.

The nuts represent something sweet and nourishing, hidden but potent. They symbolize hidden wisdom and are associated with the Maiden aspect of the Triple Goddess who brings fertility, poetry and creativity. If you find two nuts in a shell this is considered to be lucky. Eat one for inspiration and return the other to the Earth.

The forked Hazel divining stick has long been used to find hidden Water. Hazel connects us to the inner realms and our Watery unconscious self.

Hazel represents the source of our creativity and was honoured as a tree that brought fertility to the intuition.

Silver snakes of knowledge are said to twine around its roots.

The Wisdom of Hazel

Hazel has a bright energy that is quick and readily available. It has a long history of helping humankind and encourages our friendship.

The Hazel's nuts contain the wisdom of the tree, reminding us to look within, to follow our heart and inner wisdom as well as our rational mind. Hazel helps us to find inspired creative solutions, bringing ideas to the surface so that we can take action and move with the changes.

The long flexible rods inspire us to be flexible in our actions and our thinking, to flow and not become rigid or stuck.

Hazel is a tree of communication through the spark of intuition. It brings healing to the split between our conscious and unconscious minds, between our inner and outer worlds. It opens the interface between the two and allows for intuition and inspiration to be readily available in our lives. The visions we act upon will change our future and transform our present. Our dreams can become our reality through creative life-enhancing solutions.

The Wood and Its Uses

Hazel was once a valuable element in rural economy, with coppiced woodland providing wood for a great variety of uses. The rods that grow from the base of the tree provide a quantity of straight poles that are long and flexible when they are fresh.

To ensure a steady supply of poles, coppice the Hazel by cutting the whole tree back to the base between November and February. Bundle the rods together and store them under a North-facing hedge to keep them damp and pliant until you need them. They will remain flexible for six months or more if they are kept out of direct sunlight.

Since prehistoric times Hazel rods have been woven into a variety of useful products, such as the panels used in the building technique known as wattle and daub. The Hazel panels were placed between Oak posts, forming the frame of the house, which was then daubed with a mixture of mud and straw and finished off with whitewash. These panels are still used today as hurdles to pen sheep and for garden fencing. Inside the house, they can be used to make an attractive screen.

The thinner rods are used for handles in basketwork and are split for weaving larger baskets or woven furniture. Coracles, used by Welsh fishermen for 3,000 years, had a basket-like frame made of Hazel rods covered with stretched hides originally, but today made of canvas.

A simple shelter called a 'bender' can be made using six to eight sturdy Hazel rods that are driven into the ground in a circle. Make a hole for each rod first using a metal spike and a lump hammer. Weave the tops together, combining opposite rods to create a dome shape. Weave the sides with eight to ten thinner rods, tying over all the joins with a strong string for extra strength.

This structure can be covered with a tarpaulin for a shelter, den or shed or covered with clear polythene to make a greenhouse. The cover needs to be roped down, with the ropes staked well to the ground.

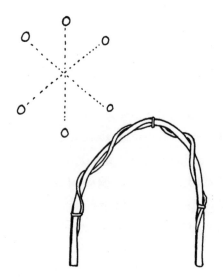

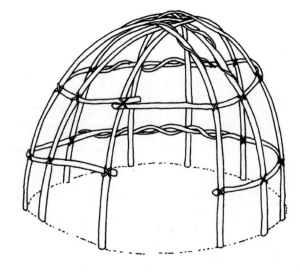

Making a Walking Stick *(see also page 268)*

A Hazel walking stick makes a good companion. It aids communication on all levels and brings about an increase in psychic abilities.

1. Sit with the tree before you cut your stick and be clear with it about what you are doing.
2. Thank the tree for its gift.
3. Trim off any side shoots and with a fine sandpaper gently sand the bark smooth and then rub in teak oil. Let it soak in and then polish the stick with a soft dry cloth.
4. Keep a psychic link between the living tree and your walking stick by visiting the tree with your stick whenever you can.

Hazel is a good choice for healing wands and talismans, helping us to overcome creative blocks and inspiring us to follow an intuitive path rather than a well thought-out plan. Hazel will stir up hidden wisdom from the depths of our psyche, bringing us new insights.

A freshly cut forked Hazel twig can be used for dowsing, especially for underground Water. Grip a fork in each hand and gently pull them apart until they are under pressure and you feel the twig 'bite'. As the twig is passed over Water, it will twitch and even sometimes twist violently in the hands. These 'V-rods' are used by geomancers to find hidden Earth energies, Water, wells or even buried treasure! The secret of success is to hold your intention clearly in your mind before you begin and to be guided by your intuitive responses.

Edible Uses: *Corylus avellana*

Hazelnuts, or 'cobs', are a rich source of protein. Collect them a little bit green in early September and store them in a warm dry place in their shells until needed. Use them in cakes, nut burgers and nut roast. Roast them in a heavy pan with a little olive oil, adding a little salt at the end and sprinkle them over any vegetarian meal.

There are no herbal uses for Hazel.

Healing Properties

Working with Hazel brings the inspiration of Brigid, the maiden Goddess of home and hearth. This creates a connection between our healing work and our daily routines. Healing needs to be rooted in our everyday lives, in the ordinary things we do, in the way we interact with everything that touches our hearts on a day-to-day basis.

Hazel facilitates deep listening, the receiving of impressions from the land, the trees, ourselves and other people. We can translate these into thoughts, words, art, music, song or poetry or any creative act, so that we can understand the wisdom we are subconsciously receiving.

Hazel brings the flame of inspiration and the active force of the vital Spirit as it joins with our natural intuitive abilities.

Spirit of
Hazel

The Earth's Cycles

The waxing and waning cycles of the Sun and the Moon provide a regular framework within which we can create ceremony, work with the Five Elements, tune in to our deepest feelings, pursue our hopes and visions and bring transformation into our lives and into the world. Connection to these cycles helps us to experience our spirituality through direct contact with the energy affecting the Earth.

Beneath the manifestation of seasonal change or the cycles of the Moon there is a subtle shift in energy that affects us all, whether we are conscious of it or not. By understanding the flow and direction of these energies, we can move in harmony with them and give ourselves the best possible conditions in which to grow, develop our spirituality and move towards the changes we wish to bring into our lives.

Whole Earth Perspective

As seen from the Earth, the Sun and Moon appear to be equal in size. The Sun is 400 times larger than the Moon but is also 400 times further away.

The Sun gives us warmth and the outward dynamic of energy for growth and self-expression. The Moon's reflective qualities distribute the Sun's energy during the hours of darkness and bring receptivity and assimilation.

The day and night cycles of the Sun and Moon occur at opposite times in the Northern and Southern Hemispheres. The natural seasonal cycles also have a mirror image in the two Hemispheres: the Summer Solstice in the Northern Hemisphere is at the same time as the Winter Solstice in the Southern Hemisphere and the Spring Equinox in one Hemisphere is balanced by the Autumn Equinox in the other.

The Moon too is the opposite way round. A waxing crescent Moon in the Northern Hemisphere faces left, while in the Southern Hemisphere it faces right.

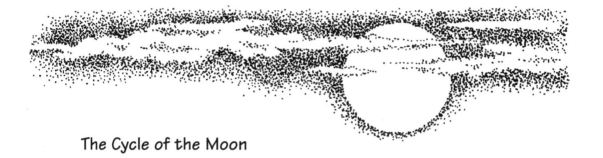

The Cycle of the Moon

The Moon is closer to the Earth than any other heavenly body and influences our lives in many ways. Her cycle of 29 days corresponds to the menstrual cycle of a woman and so in the past our ancestors personified her as a Triple Moon Goddess: the new Moon was the young Maiden, full of emerging potential, the full Moon was the Mother, the abundant provider, and the dark of the Moon was the Crone, the guardian of the inner realms and wisdom.

Everything that flows on the Earth moves in rhythm with the Moon. The force of her gravitational pull is so powerful that she influences all the Water on the Earth, the oceans' tides, the underground Waters deep in the Earth, the life fluids of plants, animals and people, all female reproductive cycles and the migration patterns of birds. The Moon can also influence our emotional patterns and our behaviour, bringing constant change to our lives.

The phase of the Moon reflects the angle between the Sun and the Moon as seen from the Earth. There are eight lunar phases and each one lasts three to four days. The Moon changes astrological Sun signs every two and a half days.

SUN

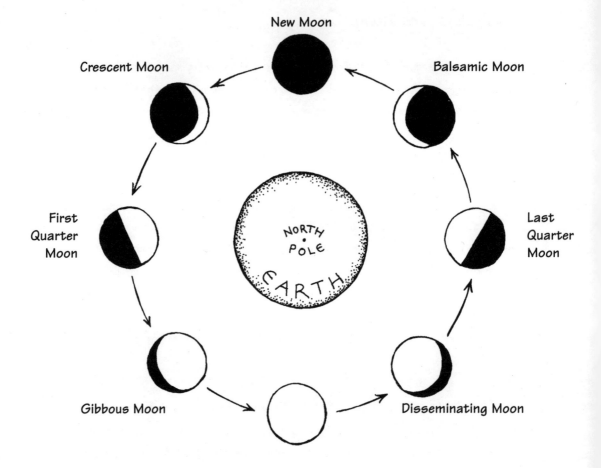

New Moon

Crescent Moon

Balsamic Moon

First
Quarter
Moon

NORTH
· POLE

EARTH

Last
Quarter
Moon

Gibbous Moon

Disseminating Moon

New Moon (Dark Moon)

Here Sun and Moon rise together in the East. The Moon is invisible because she is hidden by the Sun's brightness in the day and is on the other side of the Earth with the Sun at night. Astrologically, the Sun and Moon are in conjunction. This means that they are linked together, mutually helpful to each other, enhancing each other's energy. Their combined energy brings the potential for new beginnings. This is the best time to begin new projects, take new directions and make new resolutions, affirmations and statements of intent. The new Moon represents the Maiden aspect of the Triple Moon Goddess. She is full of potential and daring. This is the seed phase. Use it for planting seeds in the Earth and for planting the seeds of ideas, future intentions and seeds of hope.

Crescent Moon (Waxing Towards Full/Waxing Crescent)

This is the first visible sliver of Moon seen in the Western sky in the late afternoon and early evening. The crescent Moon brings new growth to ideas and plans. This is the sprouting phase.

First Quarter Moon (Waxing Half-Moon)

She rises at noon and sets at midnight. Astrologically, the Moon is square to the Sun. This is challenging energy which, if faced, will propel things forward. This is the growth phase, as the Moon is waxing towards full.

Gibbous Moon (Almost Full)

She rises mid-afternoon and sets just before dawn. This is a time for activity and personal expression through our feelings.

Full Moon

She rises at sunset and sets at sunrise and astrologically the Sun and Moon are in opposition. This means that their energies are diametrically opposite, polarizing or complementary, and this can cause mood swings and emotional turmoil. Sacred to the Mother aspect of the Triple Moon Goddess, the full Moon brings abundance and represents the flowering, the peak of fullness. Use this time for completion, self-expression and celebration.

Disseminating Moon (Waning Full Moon)

The Moon now begins to wane, visibly getting smaller each night. She rises mid-evening and sets mid-morning. In Nature the waning Moon cycle promotes root development and the swelling of fruit. She brings self-assessment and turning within.

Last Quarter Moon (Waning Half-Moon)

She rises around midnight and sets around noon. Astrologically, the Moon is square to the Sun, creating a challenge in their relationship. This is the harvest phase of the Moon, a time for reaping the fruits of our wisdom, for assimilation and quiet reflection.

Balsamic Moon (Waning Crescent Moon)

This is the last sliver of Moon seen in the Eastern sky at dawn when she rises and is visible until she sets in the early afternoon. The waning Moon is sacred to the Crone or Wise Woman aspect of the Triple Moon Goddess, bringing inner wisdom, guidance and the mysteries. This is the time for letting go of things that are no longer helpful to you, for breaking psychic links, shedding the old so that you can begin anew. Use this time for transformation and change.

The
Wheel of
the Year
and the
Cycle of
the Sun

Northern Hemisphere

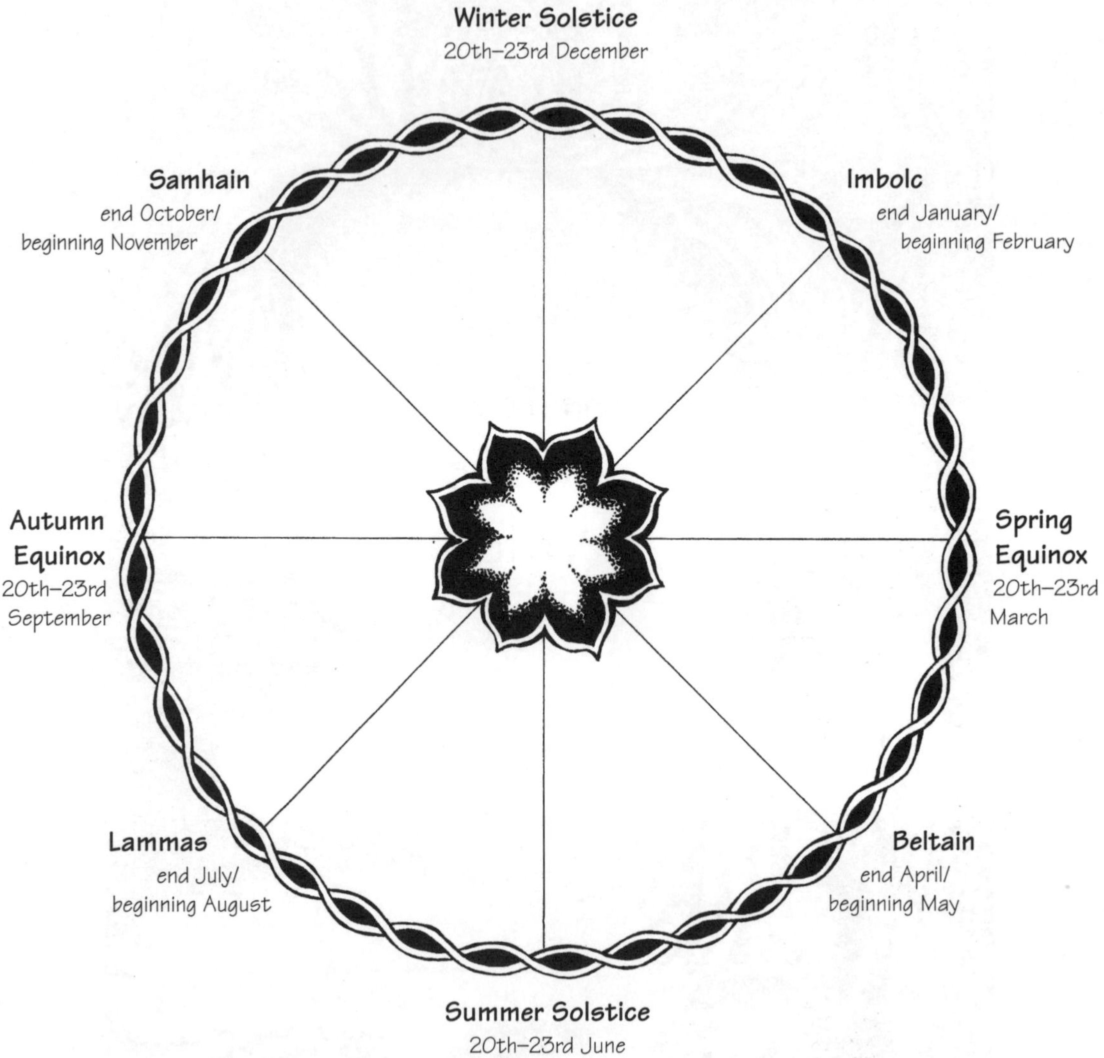

Winter Solstice
20th–23rd December

Samhain
end October/
beginning November

Imbolc
end January/
beginning February

**Autumn
Equinox**
20th–23rd
September

**Spring
Equinox**
20th–23rd
March

Lammas
end July/
beginning August

Beltain
end April/
beginning May

Summer Solstice
20th–23rd June

Southern Hemisphere

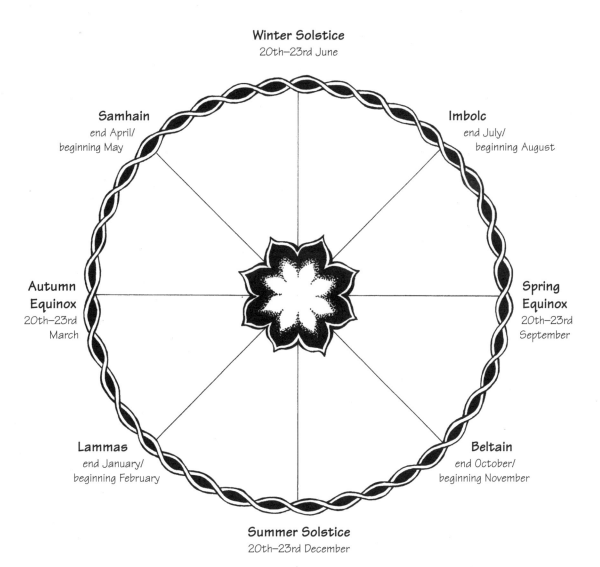

Winter Solstice
20th–23rd June

Samhain
end April/
beginning May

Imbolc
end July/
beginning August

**Autumn
Equinox**
20th–23rd
March

**Spring
Equinox**
20th–23rd
September

Lammas
end January/
beginning February

Beltain
end October/
beginning November

Summer Solstice
20th–23rd December

The Summer and Winter Solstices and the Autumn and Spring Equinoxes are the four Quarter points, the seasonal midpoints of Spring and Summer, Autumn and Winter.

In between each of the four Quarter points are the four Cross-Quarter festivals, the seasonal beginnings, known as Imbolc, Beltain, Lammas and Samhain.

Our ancestors celebrated these eight points in the yearly cycle of the Sun and used them as a framework for their lives. Here in the 21st century we do not necessarily need to experience this system as our ancestors did in the past, but the energy pattern remains the same now as it was then and we can connect with it in new ways that are relevant to us at this moment. We can either create our own personal connections, working alone, or we can meet up with friends and family, bringing community into our lives. Working with the Wheel of the Year, in whatever way, is to connect to an ancient system of Earth awareness and through it we become integrated into the natural flow of the Earth's cycle.

The eight Celtic festivals provide an opportunity every six weeks to link to the cycle of the seasons, to review what we have been doing, understand what we have learned from our experiences and focus on what we want to encourage or change in our lives. By focusing on ourselves in this way we become much clearer about who we are and create closer connections to the Earth.

From Summer Solstice the energy begins to drop down from the dizzy heights of the growing season and gradually begins to turn within. Seeds fall, leaves fall, the days shorten and all of life naturally begins to retreat within. Everything dies back and returns to the Earth. This is the composting phase of the Earth's year, providing nutrition for the new seeds which will grow in the Spring. This is also the time when roots grow in the dark of the Earth and provide a firm foundation for new growth.

The Autumn is a time to cast off the importance placed on outer achievements, to shed what is no longer helpful to us, as the plants cast off their leaves. In the Autumn we can look at what we have harvested on a personal level and we can take our new seeds of understanding and future personal growth into the dark of the Winter months and do all we can to ensure they have the best possible conditions for their future growth.

Winter is a time to rest and renew our energy. As the new year turns, our seeds are ready to be reborn. We can birth them into the new cycle by naming them as New Year resolutions or Winter Solstice solutions.

As the energy of the Spring brings forth new life in the world of Nature, we too are ready to give birth to new aspects of ourselves, new projects, new visions. We are ready to use the natural energy of outer growth to manifest change in our lives.

The Quarter Points

The four Quarter points are the Summer and Winter Solstices and the Spring and Autumn Equinoxes. These fixed points of the year's cycle form the symbol of a cross within a circle. This ancient symbol represents the wholeness, balance and stability of the Earth.

The Quarter points are in the middle of each of the seasons and are an opportunity to experience the season at its height. After this the energy of the Earth begins to change and a new season will start to emerge.

The Solstices

Solstice means 'standing of the Sun'. The two Solstices are the two great turning points of the year that keep the Earth in balance. They mark the moment when each waxing cycle reaches its peak and stops. From this point the opposite cycle begins to increase.

The waxing cycle of the Sun takes us to the longest day at Midsummer, the Summer Solstice and the height of the outward growth energy. The waning cycle of the Sun brings us to the shortest day at Midwinter, the Winter Solstice and the height of the energy that flows within.

In the Northern Hemisphere, the Winter Solstice falls between 20th and 23rd December, the Summer Solstice between 20th and 23rd June.

In the Southern Hemisphere, the Winter Solstice falls between 20th and 23rd June, the Summer Solstice between 20th and 23rd December.

Summer Solstice

At Midsummer the expanding outer cycle of the year reaches the longest day and shortest night. All of life is pulsing with outer growth and manifest energy. All beings are out in the world, celebrating their own identity and uniqueness.

At the Summer Solstice we celebrate our outer achievements and life itself.

This connection to the high point of the year brings us full circle as we look back over the year we have had. But the Solstices are a dual celebration, for at the same time as we celebrate the height of one cycle we are also acknowledging its end and the beginning of a new cycle. At the Summer Solstice we also celebrate the return of the dark and a reconnection to the wisdom within.

The light gradually decreases between the Summer Solstice and the Winter Solstice. Nature gradually withdraws from the outer world. It is time to begin exploring the inner realms, seeking rest and renewal in the dark of the year. We can use this time to form strong roots to anchor and nurture our ideas and visions.

Winter Solstice

The Winter Solstice once again brings a shift in energy as we reach the shortest day and longest night of Midwinter. Here we celebrate and honour our inner journey, the insights and wisdom we have gained. This is another dual celebration. From now on the days will begin to lengthen and so we also celebrate the return of the light, rebirth and new beginnings. We name our intentions for the new year, once again looking outwards, bringing forth the understanding gained from the journey within.

The Equinoxes

The Spring and Autumn Equinoxes are the other two Quarter points of the yearly cycle. Here day and night are of equal length. They are the balancing points between the extreme energy of the Solstices, providing an opportunity for us to unite our unconscious with our conscious mind, intuition with action. This unites our whole selves and brings balance into our lives.

The Equinoxes fall in the middle of the Spring and the Autumn, when things are beginning to move fast. Transition and change sometimes bring chaos as we adjust to new possibilities and new opportunities. We can use the balancing energy of the Equinoxes to find inner harmony so that we are prepared for the challenges of change.

In the Northern Hemisphere, the Spring Equinox falls between 20th and 23rd March and the Autumn Equinox between 20th and 23rd September.

In the Southern Hemisphere, the Spring Equinox falls between 20th and 23rd September and the Autumn Equinox between 20th and 23rd March.

The Cross-Quarter Festivals

The Cross-Quarter points fall approximately six weeks after the Quarter points, when a new season is just beginning. The new season has barely begun to show, but this is the best time to work with the developing energy.

The celebration of the Cross-Quarter festivals is not fixed by the calendar date. They are celebrated according to any relevant astrological information, most importantly the position of the Moon, and we can choose a time when these influences are at their most potent.

Celebrating the Cross Quarters can last for several days or even weeks. In the past they were known as the Four Great Fire Festivals and huge community bonfires were lit on the hilltops, uniting communities in a common focus and celebration of their lives and the Earth.

Imbolc is the Cross-Quarter festival after the Winter Solstice. In the Northern Hemisphere it falls at the end of January/beginning of February. In the Southern Hemisphere it is at the end of July/beginning of August. Here we start to see the first signs of Spring. The time is potent with the rising energy of the Earth and we can use this to bring forth our inner wisdom and inspiration and plant the seeds of our future growth.

Beltain is the Cross-Quarter festival after the Spring Equinox. In the Northern Hemisphere it falls at the end of April/beginning of May. In the Southern Hemisphere it falls at the end of October/beginning of November. It celebrates the fertility and union of all life on Earth and marks the beginning of the rampant growth of Summer.

Lammas is the Cross-Quarter festival after the Summer Solstice. In the Northern Hemisphere it falls at the end of July/beginning of August. In the Southern Hemisphere it falls at the end of January/beginning of February. This is a time of tribal gatherings, feasting, assessing the year and celebrating the beginning of the harvest season.

Samhain is the Cross-Quarter festival that falls after the Autumn Equinox. In the Northern Hemisphere it falls at the end of October/beginning of November. In the Southern Hemisphere it falls at the end of April/beginning of May. This marks the beginning of Winter, the darkest time of the year. Here we celebrate the power of regeneration, rest and renewal.

Celebrating the Earth's cycles
awakens memories deep within us
that help us to regain our commitment
to Love, respect and honour the Earth. Through
following our own unique spiritual path we learn to
find inner stillness, so that we can listen to the
land and our hearts once again.

Ash

Fraxinus excelsior

'Tree of connection to all cycles of existence'

Ash is a tall tree of imposing grace. It is not a tree for a small garden, although Ash trees can be coppiced, cut back to the base, to ensure a plentiful supply of straight rods for use in the garden or for firewood.

Ash is the 5th tree of the Celtic Tree Ogham. It represents interlinking cycles of existence and is a key to the universal understanding that all things are connected and every action has a reaction. It is associated with both the Sun and the Moon.

Ash bark is smooth and grey and the Winter twigs are distinctive because of their black horseshoe-shaped scars. In the Spring, these form the black flower buds from which the flowers and then the leaves will grow. Ash is one of the last trees to open its leaves in Spring and one of the first to drop them in Autumn. In Autumn the bunches of seeds, or 'keys', hang in bright lime-yellow clusters, maturing in October, when they turn brown.

Growing Ash Trees

Propagation of the Ash is only by seed. Pick the mature brown keys in October. Separate the individual seeds and stratify (*see Rowan, page 73*), for at least two Winters.

Folklore and Legend

In the past Ash was revered as the Tree of Life, the Cosmic Tree or World Tree, with its branches stretching far into the Heavens, its trunk in the middle world of the Earth and its roots reaching deep into the Underworld. In Northern European legend it was known as the axis of the world, Yggdrasil, which formed a link between the gods, the Earth and the world of the dead. The god Odin hung from Yggdrasil to gain illumination and hidden knowledge and to understand the runes. Yggdrasil had eagles at the top of its branches and serpents at its roots, where there was a spring or well called the Spring of Fate. Here dwelt the three legendary maidens, the Norns or Weird or Wyrd sisters, who controlled the fates of all the worlds.

Ash is linked to the Moon and the element of Water, so enhancing the intuitive flow and deep inner wisdom. It is also linked to the Sun, bringing action and stimulation. The union of the Sun and Moon brings a fusion of the human Spirit and the intuition. Odin, finding two Ash trunks on the seashore, turned them into the first woman and the first man.

In Celtic myth, the Ash was sacred to Gwydion, Welsh bard and magician and king of the British Celts. Many of his legends were absorbed into the Arthurian legends. Ash was known as the tree of enchantment from whose twigs he made his wands, and links the three circles of existence: past, present and future. This is the basis of the Celtic understanding of life as a continuous cycle of birth, death and rebirth.

The Wisdom of Ash

Ash reminds us of the connecting force of all life, in all the worlds, both seen and unseen. It teaches us to look at life from a greater perspective and to seek Oneness with the whole. It helps us realize that everything we do influences the whole of life. Our thoughts and our actions form an endless chain of events in both the material world and the Spirit world.

The Ash helps us to connect to the wisdom of the past, bringing inspiration into the present and creating a connection to the future.

It also helps us to connect to our deep inner wisdom, to life below the surface, as experienced in our dreams and inner visions. These help us to understand ourselves on a different level, beyond words and beyond reason, expanding our horizons, our visions and our minds.

Ash is associated with both Sun and Moon, Fire and Water, our rational and intuitive selves. It brings a balanced perspective and helps us to reclaim our ability to act on our intuition.

The Wood and Its Uses

Ash is a quick-growing white wood that is very tough. It is used for handles of all striking tools, such as hammers and axes, and for sports equipment such as hockey sticks, tennis rackets, skis and cricket stumps. In the past it was used for spears, bows and arrow shafts.

It steams well and is used for bentwork in furniture making and boat building. It is not good for house construction, as it decays easily on contact with damp soil conditions. It is good for turned bowls and platters, for broom handles and walking sticks.

Coppice Ash in the Autumn when the sap has returned to the roots and the leaves have fallen. Cut it right back to the base. This will encourage many new shoots to form and these will grow quickly into straight poles with many garden uses.

Ash is an excellent firewood, which even burns green.

The Druids carved Ash roots, believing their energy to be very potent. It is a valued wood for healing wands and talismans, especially potent when it has the natural spiral formed by Honeysuckle growing up it.

Ash will act as a guide to all the worlds of existence, leading you into Dreamtime and out again. It will help you to internalize and interpret your visions and intuitive impressions.

Herbal and Edible Uses: *Fraxinus excelsior*

Ash is a folk remedy for warts. Prick the wart with a clean new pin and thrust it into an Ash tree, saying, 'Ashen tree, Ashen tree, please take this wart from me'. Warts, like many growths, seem to come and go on their own and demonstrate the power of our beliefs and minds to heal our bodies.

The Fruit

An infusion (*see page 35*) of Ash keys makes a gentle but effective laxative. Ash keys can be pickled, but choose only the smallest and youngest green keys.

Healing Properties

Ash helps us to reconnect to the knowledge of the past, bringing inspiration through to the present. We are able to celebrate life on all levels and experience unity and a natural understanding of spirituality. We are able to connect to deeper levels of ourselves, without our fear, negative conditioning and self-imposed isolation holding us back from our inner truth. We are able to balance our rational minds with our intuition to gain a more holistic, healthy outlook on life.

Meditate with the Ash when you need to connect to past actions or a past life. Ask for links to hidden knowledge to help bring understanding of your present actions. Ash will aid in the process of healing the inner child. It will help create new patterns to bring about positive change in the future and affirm new beliefs in the present.

Spirit of Ash

Part
Two

Be Here Now

The second part of this book provides a framework for seasonal
activities through the eight Celtic festivals. These create an
opportunity every six weeks to align our lives to the natural rhythm of
the Earth. These eight festivals are part of a continuous cycle without
beginning or end. It doesn't matter how or where you start. Begin by
exploring what makes sense to you and see where this leads you.

The suggestions I have offered here are guidelines and inspiration for
beginning. They are for you to develop and explore, change and add
to. Every suggestion is interchangeable and open to transformation!
There are some suggestions for open events of celebration that
bring community, family and friends together. There are some
suggestions for ceremony, which brings deeper levels of spiritual
connection into our lives and our friendships.

Each festival has a chant. These spread organically and new
tunes and new words are added along the way. Sing them in rounds,
create harmonies, change them, create new ones and enjoy the good
feeling of singing together. Each section also gives some ideas for
creative projects that encourage our actions and spirituality and
affirm our positive experience of the Earth.

*Our health and spiritual well-being are enhanced by communication as we share
our feelings and understanding with each other. It is important that we accept
and support each person's unique and personal spiritual path so that everyone
feels included and respected for who they are and who they are becoming.*

Samhain

'Festival of the Year's End and New Beginnings'
End of October/beginning of November in the Northern Hemisphere
End of April/beginning of May in the Southern Hemisphere

Samhain (pronounced 'sow'eine') marks the end and the beginning of the Celtic year. All of life is part of a cycle and here we acknowledge the new beginning in the midst of endings.

All of life is withdrawing inside itself now. This is Autumn's end and the beginning of Winter. Increasing cold and dark are forcing us to adjust to the end of the old year. Once we accept this and let go of our attachment to it, a new set of possibilities is revealed. There is a new power to life as we nurture new dreams and new seeds in the dark. By accepting this period of rest, we find rejuvenation and renewal.

This is not a time for action but a time to drift, to dream, to vision and remember. It is a time for meditation and welcoming inner stillness, for long-term plans and for nourishing our Spirit.

Here as the old year ends and the darkness of Winter begins, we welcome the opportunity for a new start as we incubate and strengthen our hopes for the new year. Traditionally, it is an opportunity to honour our ancestors and embrace our roots.

Samhain has always been seen as a magical time. The veil between the seen world of matter and the unseen world of Spirit becomes thin, especially at dawn and dusk. This creates opportunities for us to slip through the fabric of space and time, beyond the limitations of our rational mind, and gain wisdom from within.

Samhain Celebration

☆ Traditionally, this is an evening celebration, with a bonfire outside. Invite friends and family to gather together, celebrate the passing of the old year and remember those who have passed on from this world.

☆ Ask everyone to bring food and drink to share, drums and percussion and wood for the fire.

☆ Make a headdress from the last of the vegetation of the old year, using pliable stems such as Ivy or Willow (see page 181). Decorate it with Autumn leaves, berries and seedheads and wear it to the celebration.

☆ Bring photos of people you feel close to who have died. These may include family, friends or even people you did not know personally but who meant a lot to you. Bring anything that reminds you of them. Also bring flowers and cloths, bowls of sand and small candles to create an ancestral shrine where these items can be placed. Light many candles in celebration of those people and their lives. Share your thoughts and feelings with each other.

☆ Ask everyone to bring things from their garden or the wild — anything that has been recently pruned and is still flexible enough to be used for weaving, as well as seedheads, berries, sweet-smelling herbs and leaves. Weave the stems together to create something that represents the Spirit of the Old Year. It may be a woven wheel, a ball or a figure. Put in a place of honour, creating a central shrine where each person can spend a few private minutes in contemplation of the passing year. It can later be burnt on the fire.

☆ The pieces of vegetation left over can be made into individual posies, tied together with ribbon, added to the central creation or be taken home at the end.

⭐ In case of rain and cold, make sure there is somewhere warm and dry where everyone can gather indoors, with tables for the food and a means of making hot drinks. Avoid electric light if possible, lighting everywhere with candle lanterns and nightlights in jars.

A chant:

'I am tomorrow's ancestor
The future of yesterday
And what I am in the here and now
goes rippling out all ways
Goes rippling out always.'

by Brian Boothby

Samhain Ceremony

⭐ Gather in a circle round the fire or, if you are indoors, light some candles in a bowl of sand and place them at the centre of the circle. Switch off the electric lights, so that all can enjoy the flickering light of the living flame. Use a steady drumbeat to gather the group together, creating an atmosphere of calm stillness. Hold hands and gently hum or chant together, resting in the power of the circle, stillness and friendship.

⭐ Open the ceremony by acknowledging each of the Five Elements in turn. Share words and images about each element so that your words help to create connections and inspiration. Welcome the ancestors into your circle. Connect to your lineage, however you perceive it to be, and name those you welcome.

☆ Hum and make sounds together that help create a meditative atmosphere. Pass round a bag of crystals that have been previously cleansed by burying them in the Earth or in salt for 24 hours. Each person chooses one and holds it in the middle of their forehead, asking that it be used as a focus for healing. Then everyone sings to their crystal at the same time, blending sounds and notes together to energize the connection. Ask the crystal for a healing symbol to work with over the Winter months and see what images come into your mind. Let the sounds gradually fade away and share with each other any healing symbols you received. Take your crystal home with you and continue to meditate and journey with it over the Winter months.

☆ If you have a fire, burn the Spirit of the Old Year that you made or put your headdress on the fire, thanking the year as it burns. Speak your gratitude out loud: 'I thank this year for…' or name what you have learned: 'This year has taught me…'

☆ If you don't have a fire, have a basket of sticks that have naturally blown from the trees. Each person takes a stick and uses it as a focus for what they wish to let go of from the old year so that everyone is free to make a new start. Say: 'I let go of…' These sticks can be burnt later or buried in the ground to aid transformation and release.

☆ Traditionally, this is mischief night and could provide a focus for some positive action that is done in a sacred manner while you are still in sacred space.

☆ Close the circle by thanking the elements and the energy they bought to the ceremony. This can be done in reverse order to the opening ceremony, unwinding the energy that was created. Thank the ancestors for their presence and wisdom.

☆ Drum and dance together in celebration of the old year passing and a new year beginning.

☆ Bless the food and drink and lay a place at the table for the ancestors or a particular ancestor, welcoming your 'guest' in the age-old tradition of Samhain.

Headdresses

Gather lengths of pliable foliage such as grasses, Ivy, Willow, Dogwood, Vine, Silver Birch, Broom, Hop and Honeysuckle.

Lay them all out with the thicker stem ends all facing in the same direction. Gently pull some of the lengths along so that the stem ends become staggered.

Weave them together to form a length of 3–6 feet (1–2 metres) and bind the whole thing with a length of Ivy or embroidery thread. Keep feeding in more lengths if needed. Make a band the size of your head by weaving the length into a circle.

Decorate the circlet by poking in clusters of berries, Autumn leaves, herbs, feathers and seedheads.

As you create your headdress, focus on the old year and your memories. Let out your emotions and tears if necessary. Wear your headdress to honour and accept the old year as part of your experience.

Ancestral Connections

Dedicate this time to the power of lineage, whether this is biological, tribal or mythical. Follow your intuitive threads and explore what you feel are your own personal connections, roots and heritage. Name and celebrate your heirloom gifts, what you feel you have inherited and what you feel you have been entrusted with.

Dedicate two stones or crystals to honour your ancestry. Keep one on your personal shrine and take one somewhere that makes a good connection for you and bury it, cast it into Water or leave it out in the elements.

As an ancestor of the next generation, ask yourself what history you leave behind.

Seeds of Beauty

Transform an eyesore into a place of beauty. Choose an area that Nature is already reclaiming — a canal bank, a piece of wasteland, an old car park or copse of trees that is littered with rubbish. Clear up the rubbish, plant some Spring bulbs and scatter some native wildflower seeds.

Vision Meditation

Here in the dark of the year, acknowledge your deep feelings of despair and hopelessness about the way our world is managed by those in power. We know that poverty, famine, war and pollution can be avoided and yet we feel overwhelmed by our powerlessness to help. Samhain is a time for transformation and we can use it to envision a better future for the world.

Sit comfortably and let your energy drop from your head into your belly. Breathe deeply and rhythmically until you feel yourself slipping into a state of meditative stillness.

Begin to visualize a worldwide community of people dedicated to inclusion and fairness for all.

Visualize a new future based on trust, cooperation and sustainability, with respect for the Earth and all her inhabitants.

Visualize how this will transform our everyday lives, businesses, governments, schools, families, children and grandchildren.

Plant this seed and nurture it, without limiting it or blocking it. Send it out into the world, full of its own power and strength.

After your meditation, commit yourself to your vision, to becoming the person who will make that vision a reality. Let go of your anxieties and sense of inadequacy and resolve to strengthen positive change in your outlook and your actions.

Inspire others! Determination is contagious! The more people join together, the more the impossible becomes possible!

Yew

Taxus baccata

'Tree of the ancestors and transformation'

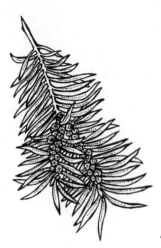

There are at least 10 different species of Yew in the Northern temperate zones of Britain, North America, Asia, Asia Minor, India and Northern Europe. As the Ice Age came to an end and the glaciers receded North, the great forests of Europe consisted of up to 80 percent of Yew trees.

Yew is the 20th tree in the Celtic Tree Ogham, representing death and rebirth, transformation, access to the ancestors and the Otherworld. It is associated with Saturn and Mercury, both elements of transformation.

The Yew has managed to survive the great climatic changes of our planet and has adapted to live longer than any other species alive today. Because of its unique way of growing new trunks from beneath the root bole, it is now estimated that some of the oldest Yew trees alive today may be 4,000 or 5,000 years old, spanning all the ages of known human history.

Yews were used as landmarks, as their size, longevity, evergreen leaves and huge spread of branches stand out well in the landscape. Yew groves, planted by the Druids, were common by ancient burial mounds, ridgeways and sacred sites. They marked ceremonial ways and linked sacred sites together.

Many ancient Yews are to be found in old forests and in churchyards. Ancient Yews and their great girths have been documented throughout history.

Growing Yew Trees

Yew trees can be propagated through cuttings , growing the seed or layering (encouraging the branch of an existing Yew to reach the ground and root). It is also possible to find many small Yew trees which have grown from seeds that have passed through birds when they have eaten the fruit. These can be dug up in the Autumn and transplanted. Yew prefers a moist fertile sandy loam, but will grow in most soils apart from waterlogged ground or wet clay.

Growing Yew Trees from Cuttings

(To take cuttings, see Elder, page 46). Cuttings of Yew taken from lateral branches generally produce shrub-like plants, while those taken from the erect top branches are more likely to produce a tree.

Warning: All parts of the Yew, except for the flesh around the seed, are poisonous and care should be taken while handling any part of this tree.

Folklore and Legend

Our ancestors revered the Yew above all other trees and it has always been associated with death and rebirth, endings of cycles and new beginnings. Yew trees were said to mark the entrance to Hel, which was not the Christian

Hell of eternal damnation but the realm of Helenes, a goddess of the Underworld. Hel was originally a uterine shrine or sacred cave of rebirth, a place of transformation and regeneration. Yew trees were held sacred to the Crone aspect of the Triple Goddess in the Celtic tradition and to Hecate, the Greek death goddess, who held dominion over the land of the dead.

Yew has long been part of funerary customs, with many variations in different districts and countries. These mainly involve carrying sprigs of Yew, which are then thrown into the grave, either on top of or under the coffin. Yew was one of the evergreens traditionally used for Winter Solstice decorations, celebrating the rebirth of life and the Sun.

Many ancient Yews can be found growing on or very near blind springs. Carvings of Yew wood have been found at the bottom of ancient wells. These are thought to be votive offerings made to the Spirit of Water.

Many ancient Yews are found in churchyards and there is no doubt that many of them were there long before the churches were built and that they mark the sacred sites of our ancestors. The tribal chiefs of our ancestors were buried under a Yew in the belief that their knowledge and wisdom would be joined with the Dryad of the Yew tree and remain accessible to the tribe.

The Wisdom of Yew

Many ancient Yews have stood in the same spot for thousands of years, forming a direct link with our past. They remind us that we all have access to the spiritual guidance of our ancestors and the Otherworld.

Yew is constantly regenerating from its own root system, teaching us the power of continuity and rebirth. This helps us to challenge the illusionary nature of life, so that we can live our lives more consciously and not fear death. Often death is fraught with a sense of loss, but Yew teaches us to view it as a form of transformation. Nothing ends, everything lives on, as life creates new life in ever-forming cycles.

The Wood and Its Uses

Yew is a slow-growing tree that produces a tight-grained wood which is tough and resilient. It is a beautiful wood, deep orange with a deep red inner core. It carves well and sands up very smoothly. It takes polish very well and creates a beautiful finish.

In the past Yew was used to make small bows, spikes and staves, the bodies of lutes, wheels and cogs, handles and boxes. It was used for the famous longbow of the Middle Ages, which made from the heartwood, the dark wood at the centre.

If you wish to make a healing wand from Yew, spend time with the tree before asking for a twig to use. The wood is considered to be very magical and in the past people used it for votive offerings and for creating a link to their ancestors.

Important: The wood and bark are poisonous. Wear a mask to avoid breathing in the dust when sanding.

Herbal Uses: *Taxus baccata*

Because the Yew is poisonous, there are no herbal or edible uses. In recent years it has been found that taxol, a chemical found in the bark of the Yew, inhibits cell growth and cell division. This may have some promise in helping find a cure for cancer. However, it takes a large amount of bark to produce a small amount of taxol and it has not been possible to produce it synthetically. Yew was used by early peoples for making weapons and for making poison, both tools of death. Now, thousands of years later, it is providing hope for cancer patients to avert death.

Healing Properties

Death heralds the end of something. It may be a physical death, the death of our old selves, an old way of life or an old way of looking at things. Yet each end, each death, is a new beginning, a new hope, a new future and an opportunity for transformation. Sometimes things need to end or die before the new can begin.

Yew can help us to overcome our fears of our own death, to progress to an understanding of the life beyond life, opening the way for hope, joy and a greater inner peace and stillness. We are constantly being reborn: each new year is born out of the old, each new part of ourselves is born out of our experiences, each new life springs from the death of the old one. Yew helps us with this process of transformation and rebirth. Healing Yew wands can be intuitively used as an aid to healing family disputes or traumas that repeat themselves over generations.

Spirit of
Yew

Winter Solstice

'The Festival of Rebirth'

20–23 December in the Northern Hemisphere

20–23 June in the Southern Hemisphere

This is Midwinter, the shortest day and longest night of the year. The restraints of Winter have brought us rest and given us time for reflection and the incubation of ideas and dreams. Here in the stillness of the Solstice we pause and become aware of our visions and the seeds of our future growth waiting for birth.

At the Winter Solstice the darkness reaches its height and the waning cycle of the Sun stops. From now on the days will begin to lengthen and warmth and outer growth will return to us and to the Earth.

Here we celebrate the return of the Sun, give birth to our visions and name our dreams, our 'Solstice Resolutions' or 'Solstice Aspirations', which will grow with the increasing light. The way is now open for the rebirth of our active selves.

But this is also a dual celebration and we pause a moment to look back on our journey since the Summer Solstice, acknowledging what we have completed and the insights and understanding we have gained from inner reflection.

The Winter Solstice is an opportunity to come out of hibernation, to be loving and generous, to reconnect and celebrate friendships, family and the warmth of community.

Winter Solstice Celebration

⊙ Dress up warmly and get up before dawn to gather with friends and watch the Sun come up over the horizon. Celebrate the rebirth of the Sun and the return of the light. Celebrate the journey you have made inside yourself and the dreams you have been incubating.

- Stay together throughout the day, inviting more friends and family to gather at noon and celebrate the day and evening together as a community. Book a hall so that all may come and join in.

- Gather evergreens, enjoying the contact with Nature and respecting the plants and trees as you cut them. Arrange all the greenery in buckets of damp soil and vases of Water, respecting the living energy of the plants. Display them in corners of the room and on the tables, with beautiful cloths and nightlights in holders around them.

- Light the room with candle lanterns and sidelights to create a special atmosphere of gentle light.

- Invite everyone to bring special food and drink to share and to bring a present for the 'present share'. Each present must be labelled and correspond to each child, teenager or adult that comes. Place these in baskets labelled 'Child', 'Teenager' and 'Adult'. At an appropriate moment during the celebration, the baskets can be brought into the centre and each person can choose their Solstice gift.

- Bring drums, percussion and instruments, as well as rugs and cushions to make a cosy area for the children to play and sleep in.

- Invite everyone to dress as the Spirit of Midwinter. This may include costumes, masks, headdresses and painted faces. It facilitates imaginative creativity and brings a special sparkle to the event.

- The Winter Solstice is traditionally a time to entertain each other, so invite everyone to bring music, songs, plays, poems and stories to share.

A chant:

'We are the rising Sun.
We are the change.
We are the ones we are waiting for and
We are dawning.'

Winter Solstice Ceremony

- ☉ Gather everyone into a circle with a chant, holding hands and circling round together, building up a connection to each other and the Solstice. Sing the chant for at least 10 minutes. This gives everyone the chance to really get to know it, to make up harmonies and play with it. After a while it slips into a mesmerizing phase, takes on a life of its own and really builds up energy. Encourage everyone to join in, from the youngest to the oldest, so that all feel included in their community.

- ☉ At the centre of the circle place a special blessed candle in a large bowl of sand, with a basket of small candles next to it. Light the central candle with a simple invocation, dedicating it to world peace or global harmony.

- ☉ Open the circle by beginning with a grounding exercise (see page 56), helping everyone to let go of their busy lives and their worries, letting everything drop down into the Earth where it will be cleansed and renewed.

⊙ Acknowledge each element in turn with music, sound, dance, song or words. This can be done by the whole group or by individuals. It may be decided on beforehand or it may unfold in the moment as an act of creative group spontaneity.

⊙ Turn off all the lights and meditate together on the stillness of the single living flame of the candle at the centre of the circle. Hum and let out gentle sounds together to facilitate a mesmerizing trance-like atmosphere.

⊙ Each person goes to the centre of the circle and names what they wish to bring to their lives, to the Earth or the world in the new year. As they do this, they take a candle from the small basket, light it from the central candle and place it in the large bowl of sand. Gradually, as each person lights their candle with pledges of hope for positive change, the room is filled with light.

⊙ Pass around a warm spicy fruit cup and let each person offer a blessing and a toast to the new year. Echo each toast by calling it out together so all can hear it and all can send it out into the world. Drink from the cup and pass it on to the next person. Encourage the children to join in and add an element of fun and daring! Make sure there is someone to refill the cup when necessary.

⊙ Close the circle by acknowledging each element in the same way as when you opened the circle, reversing the order if this makes sense to you. Drum and dance together in celebration of each other, your community and the rebirth of the Sun.

⊙ Have a great Solstice feast together and entertain each other with music, plays, stories and songs.

Space Clearing

When we spend a lot of time indoors during the Winter months, the atmosphere in our living spaces can become cluttered and clogged with emotional and psychic residue. It can hold imprints of energy from past events, especially if there have been emotionally charged situations such as arguments or unhappiness. Space clearing is a very effective way to clear out the old stale energy and re-energize the room.

Begin by gathering together something from each of the elements, such as a bell or chimes for Air, a candle or burning sage for Fire, a bowl of blessed spring water for Water or a plant spray of spring Water with a few drops of Lavender oil or an appropriate flower remedy added, and a bowl of rock salt, sand or soil to represent Earth.

Ground yourself before you begin, breathing deeply and meditating on your intention to clear and re-energize the space.

When you feel ready, choose a place to begin, laying out your elements on a cloth or scarf. Clear out all the things from the room that can be washed, especially crystals, which can also hold imprints of energy. Open the window to let in some fresh Air.

Begin with the bells or chimes and ring them all around the room, paying attention to the corners, where stale energy becomes trapped. You might sing or feel moved to tone certain notes. You might say something like 'By the power of Air I cleanse this space'. Do whatever feels good to you and picture the energy breaking up and dissipating. Spend extra time in any areas where the atmosphere feels 'sticky', until you feel it change and become clear.

Take up each element in turn, following your intuition as you use each one.

Finally, close the window, put fresh flowers or greenery in Water, light a candle and replace all the washed crystals and artefacts. The difference you have made in the atmosphere is felt immediately.

Shrines and Altars

These are found in all spiritual practices the world over and are created as a focus for the sacred.

A personal shrine or altar is a place for reflective contemplation and helps us to keep our spiritual connections vibrant and alive. Shrines or altars can be created inside or outside, in a place central to family life or in a quiet corner of a bedroom. Define the space by a special cloth and place anything here that reminds you of what is important on your spiritual path at this time. You can add anything that you wish to honour or bless, such as things from Nature, talismans, healing wands, crystals, photos or a dedicated candle.

You can also create seasonal shrines to honour each of the eight Celtic festivals, adding seasonal symbols, colours and objects from Nature at each festival.

As part of your Solstice decorations, create a shrine dedicated to the Winter Solstice. Bring to it all that has meaning for you at this time, what is emerging for you and what you wish to remember and honour during the coming weeks. At Imbolc, change it to reflect the next new season, connecting to the change of energy inherent in this, and so on. Each festival brings a new opportunity to create a new shrine and prepare for the new energy that is emerging.

To make a shrine is to make a sacred connection to your spirituality and inner understanding. Take some quiet time for yourself as you create what has meaning for you.

If you are creating a new indoor shrine, wash everything beforehand.

Each element and its direction may be represented in whatever way feels good to you. The symbols can be placed on a circular mirror or circular wooden board to remind you of the cyclic nature of all natural cycles. An empty vessel or candle may be placed at the centre to represent Spirit; feathers, chimes or a bell in the East to represent Air; a candle or incense in the South to represent Fire; a bowl of spring water in the West to represent Water; and a vase of greenery, flowers, crystals, a bowl of soil or rock salt in the North to represent Earth. If you do use rock salt, change it frequently, as salt absorbs impurities.

From time to time completely dismantle your shrine area, re-energize it by space clearing around it (see page 160) and wash everything. If possible, let everything dry in the Sun and the wind and charge crystals up in the Sun and by the light of the Full Moon.

Outdoor shrines can be built in your garden and used for contemplation and connection to your spiritual practice and to Nature. They may be dedicated to any of the Five Elements, to the ancestors, to the Moon, to the faerie folk, to the Spirit of Nature, to world peace or to anything that inspires you.

With all shrines, indoor or outside, frequent use keeps their energy vibrant and alive.

Dream Incubation

Winter is a good time to turn inwards and connect to our dream world.

Dreams defy our logical minds and yet can bring us insights into ourselves, answers to our problems, inspiration and even forewarnings. They were once looked upon as oracles, messages from the gods, angels, the ancestors or Spirit. They were considered to be important for gaining access to other aspects of our psyche, and interpreting them was an art and an act of divination.

Dream incubation is an ancient tradition of focusing on a request or question before you go to sleep.

During the day use your conscious intellect to help you be clear about your question. The clearer it is, the more clearly you can interpret your dream. Write it down on a piece of paper. According to ancient dream lore, this should be placed under the pillow on the night you intend to incubate the dream.

Before you go to bed, meditate on your intention and your question so that it is firm and clear. Place a pen and notebook by your bed.

Dedicate your sleep to incubation, saying a prayer to ask for help with your question or problem.

Just before you go to sleep is the best time to focus on your quest, while in a state of relaxed alertness.

As soon as you wake up, write down everything you remember and think about the interpretation later.

Interpreting Dreams

- ☽ When interpreting dreams, keep your analysis on the content of the dream, not your place within it.
- ☽ Begin by focusing on the theme of the dream and what this could represent. You might try viewing the dream as if it were a play or a painting. Give it a title.
- ☽ Read your account of your dream, asking the same question: 'What could this scene symbolically represent?'. Stay focused on this until it becomes clear.
- ☽ Next take into consideration the mood of the dream and the feeling that it left you with.
- ☽ Finally, when the theme and content of the dream have been thoroughly explored, then they can be applied to your circumstances or question.

Holly

Ilex aquifolium

'Tree of restored direction'

Holly is one of our best-known evergreen native trees and is found in hedgerows and gardens all over Europe. It is slow-growing, tolerates shade well and is often found in the understorey of woodlands.

Holly is the 8th tree of the Celtic Tree Ogham, representing restored balance, restored direction, Unconditional Love and increased detachment from emotional turmoil. Ruled by Mars, it provides the raw energy to get things done.

The Holly tree flowers in June, when the leaves are soft, but during the Winter, when the evergreen Holly is likely to be attacked by browsing animals, the leaves harden and the spikes appear. Only the female trees have the bright red berries, which are eaten by birds throughout the Winter months.

Growing Holly Trees

Collect the red berries from the tree in Winter and remove the seeds from the flesh by washing them thoroughly. Soak the berries for a day or two if the flesh is hard to remove. Stratify the seeds for one or two Winters (*see Rowan, page 73*).

Folklore and Legend

Evergreen Holly is a potent symbol of the life force in the depths of the Winter. Symbolizing everlasting life, it is used for Winter Solstice and Christmas decorations. Many different customs have survived in different areas regarding the use of Holly for decorations, but the most important thing to remember is to cut the Holly with heartfelt respect for the tree.

Customs regarding disposal of the Holly twigs afterwards vary too, such as burning them or returning them to the Earth. Sometimes a small branch is kept until the following year to bring continuity in luck.

Holly is associated with both female and male and in former times care was taken to bring equal amounts of prickly Holly and smooth Holly into the house. The prickly Holly was good for men and the smooth Holly was the she-Holly, good for women. The red berries are associated with the female blood of life and the more berries, the more good fortune for the year ahead. The male aspect is linked in legend to the Green Man and the Green Knight, who represents the testing of the Spirit.

Holly has always been regarded as a tree of great strength, a positive force that brings balance and restored direction. Throughout our folklore, it is a symbol of justice and steadfastness in adversity. It was often used symbolically on badges and in heraldry, especially in the Scottish clans.

The Holly King represents a great spiritual warrior, ready to protect the natural world at the most vulnerable time of the year. He fights alongside the

Oak King at Midwinter and Midsummer and is the guardian of the two great turning points of the year and a symbol of transformation.

Traditionally, Holly was planted near the house to bring protection from evil, disturbed spirits, poisoned thoughts and lightning. As it was considered to be a tree of good fortune, it was thought to be unlucky to cut it down.

The Wisdom of Holly

Holly represents the potency of the life force in the midst of darkness. It brings a balanced power that will guide us towards positive action.

All negative emotions greatly weaken the life force by causing constant inner turmoil. They create negative patterns of thought which affect the body and cause illness. When we are aware of the repercussions that our negative emotions can have on those around us, we learn to accept responsibility for our actions.

Holly encourages us to communicate and express our feelings, to bring things out into the open, so that resolution is possible. Its message is to direct your thoughts wisely, to resolve any problems by open communication and a loving outlook.

Holly is a tree that brings transformation and restored direction. It represents Fire in the Spirit, the power of our will to bring change for the good of all.

The Wood and Its Uses

Holly is a hard dense white wood. It is difficult to dry, as it distorts, and once dry it can move in changing humidity. It takes stain well and is known as 'English ebony' when it is dyed black and used as an ebony substitute. It is particularly used for carving, turning and inlay. It sands and polishes well, producing a smooth, almost bone-like finish.

In the past Holly was used for spears and arrows, which were believed to fly straight and true.

As firewood it burns very hot.

It is possible to find straight Holly sticks for making staffs and walking sticks. Touchwoods for the pocket and wands can be made from the Holly cut for Solstice decorations. These can be used to help restore inner harmony in times of emotional turmoil.

Herbal Uses: *Ilex aquifolium*

Leaves

These are best collected in May and June by gathering them into brown paper bags. Reject any leaves that are stained or marked by insects.

Make an infusion (*see page 35*) and drink it as a tea for colds, catarrh and influenza and as an expectorant for persistent coughs. Holly is a useful diuretic for any urinary infection and can be used to eliminate toxins from the body and to prevent kidney stones. If taken hot it will encourage sweating and bring down fevers.

Bark and Leaves

These can be made into a poultice that can be used to help set a broken bone (see page 35).

Berries

Warning: The berries are mildly poisonous to children. They may cause vomiting and diarrhoea.

For adults, a few ripe berries may be eaten as a strong purgative, to clear the body of unwanted waste or toxins.

Holly Flower Remedy

This will help those whose emotions have become out of control, with feelings of hatred, jealousy, envy and suspicion and thoughts of revenge. It is useful for those who have become oversensitive, always finding fault with others, and for those who are irritable with people around them. These feelings may not be outwardly revealed, but Holly will help the emotions to come to the surface, aiding communication and restoring balance.

Holly flower remedy also aids the flow of the positive life force, so that we can move beyond our negative emotions to reach a place where we can Love and respect ourselves and move on to Love and respect others.

Healing Properties

Holly brings a balanced power which will guide our actions towards Unconditional Love and compassion and an increased detachment from emotional turmoil.

It also brings the power of directed thought. We can use this wisely to send out messages of Love and healing, especially to those whom we find challenging or emotionally difficult. Sending positive messages out into the world will also help to spread peace and harmony through our shared collective thoughts.

Spirit of
Holly

Imbolc

'Festival of Awakening'

End of January/beginning of February in the Northern Hemisphere

End of July/beginning of August in the Southern Hemisphere

Now we become aware that the Earth is no longer still but stirring. What has been curled up begins to unfurl; the first buds are swelling on the trees and Spring bulbs are pushing up through the Earth. Our acceptance of Winter is giving way to an urge to move forward and become active once again.

Now is the time to express our creativity through art, craft, poetry and songs, accessing ancestral memory and inner wisdom. We can use this time to prepare for the changes ahead and to bring visions and insights out into the returning light.

This is the time for initiation and healing, for reclaiming what has been lost and seeking new ways forward. It is a time for working with our intuition, for acting on inspired leaps of understanding and for expressing our deepest wishes, beliefs and feelings. Be open to communication from within, heed the signs and omens when you notice them and follow what has significance to you.

Imbolc reflects the stirring of the life force, the potency of action that is fired from within and the power of Fire to transform and energize. It is sacred to the Muses, to Love, to the young fertile force in all of us, to the quickening of new life and new beginnings.

Imbolc Celebration

Gather with friends at the new Moon when the Moon energy is also fertile and rising. Ask everyone to bring a candle, food and drink to share and their own poems, songs, artwork, craftwork or any Winter project they wish to celebrate, so that everyone can share in each other's accomplishments and uniqueness. Bring drums, percussion and instruments to play.

◊ Ask those who can to bring fresh cuttings of stems that can be woven, such as Willow, Winter Jasmine, Honeysuckle, Forsythia, Dogwood, Flowering Red Currant, Almond and Cherry. Lay them on an old sheet or blanket (for ease of clearing up at the end) and sit around this to weave an 'Imbolc ring'.

To begin, choose a long length and with the thicker end of the stem create a circle the size of a plate. Use the thin end like a needle, weaving it in and out until it holds firm as a ring.

Continue weaving in different twigs, anchoring the thick end into the circle first and weaving with the thin end, until you build up a ring of different plants. As you work, focus on what you have learned during the Winter months and where you wish to take this as the new active season begins.

Imbolc rings can be taken home and placed in a shallow dish of Water. Over the next few weeks they will leaf and flower, giving energy to your visions and new directions.

◊ Sit together to share your poems, songs and achievements.

A chant:

'We are the power in everyone.
We are the dance of the Moon and the Sun.
We are the hope that will never hide.
We are the turning of the tide.'

Imbolc Ceremony

- ◊ Gather everyone together with a chant or song around a central large bowl of soil or compost, which is piled high in celebration of the fertile force of the Earth. Place unlit candles around this, each in a small bowl of sand, one for each person.

- ◊ Begin with a grounding exercise, breathing deeply down into the Earth, letting go of any problems or worries, letting them fall away into the Earth so that they can rest and be transformed.

- ◊ Open the circle by bringing focus to each of the elements and their awakening energy at this time. This can be done by focusing on the power and beauty of each element and spontaneously sharing any words and images that come to mind. Use these to create a new chant together, keeping it short and simple so it is easy to learn.

- ◊ Lead the circle into a spiral, circling round the unlit candles and bowl of Earth at the centre, singing the new elemental chant.

- ◊ Stop at the centre and focus silently on what seeds you have been nurturing and what you wish to plant in the fertile energy of this newly emerging season. Symbolically plant them in the bowl of Earth and as you do so, let out sounds and notes that resonate with those seed wishes and intentions. Let all the sounds resonate together in a cone of power and vibrant energy.

- ◊ Spiral back out again, reconnecting to the elemental chant.

- ◊ Once everyone is back in the circle, each person goes to the centre and lights their candle as they name and celebrate their seed wishes.

- ◊ Close the circle by thanking each element for the part it will play in the new growing season.

◊ Drum and dance together, releasing your inner Fire into the fertile power of the life force.

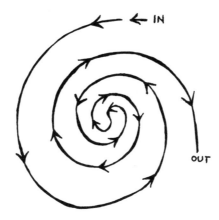

Spiral dance

Actions with Heart

Imbolc is the best time for initiating change and giving life to our ideas, visions and flashes of insight. Whatever we set in motion now will expand as the new season of active growth and manifestation begins.

Work with the power of goodwill and goodness as a potent force for change. Light a candle every day for the power of goodwill, inventing actions that could spread goodwill and goodness throughout the world. Let others know any ideas you have for this, so that these seed ideas can grow. Imagine the world becoming a more heart-centred place as you visualize Love as an unstoppable force that will fill the world with its strength.

Use the spark of Fire, the active principle, to bring energy and passion to your visions for a better world. Sometimes we need to take risks, to sacrifice the old so that the new has room to grow.

Be a catalyst for change. No matter how small your action, every single positive thing will add to the whole. Do something that makes a difference! Inspire others to do the same! Whatever you dream you can do, do it now!

Light a candle for each person who comes into your dreams, thoughts or life at this time. Without judgement or prejudice, send them Love and picture goodwill spreading into their lives.

Wells and Springs

This is the traditional time to make a pilgrimage to a healing well, holy well or spring. The power of Water can be used to bring fertility and healing to our hopes and dreams. Some wells and springs have a special tree connected to them. In the past, a pilgrim seeking healing would soak a rag from their clothing and tie it to the tree. As the rag rotted away, they believed their illness would disappear. This practice could be revived using 'pledge' or 'prayer' ribbons.

Take a piece of ribbon with you, dip it into the Water as you state your pledge or prayer for change, and tie it to the tree. Here it will flutter in the wind, like a prayer flag, carrying messages of hope and healing.

Use the Water for baptism, as a rite of passage, to wash away the past,

the Winter or the old 'you'. Use it to bless a new beginning, to bring healing, to energize an affirmation or an intention.

When you leave, thank the Water and leave an offering to the Spirit of the place and the Spirit Guardian of the well. This may be something made of clay or wood, a crystal, some fruit or nuts or a pattern you make from the natural materials you find nearby. One of the best gifts you can give is to clear up any rubbish you find there and take it away with you.

Trees

Make the most of the pale sunlight to get outside and reconnect to the awakening Earth. There is still time to plant or move young trees before the growing season gathers momentum. Plant a new fruit tree and dedicate it to someone or to a project. There are many dwarf varieties that can even be grown in a large pot if space is limited.

Coppice Willows and Dogwoods, having enjoyed their brightly coloured stems during the Winter months. Save these for woven projects in the garden by storing them bundled together on a North-facing hedgerow to keep them pliant. Plant them straight into the Earth to grow living woven fences or Willow dens or to grow new trees.

A Moon Garden

Start plans for creating a Moon garden, a place to sit in quiet contemplation and make a connection to the Watery flow of your unconscious mind, especially during the active half of the year. If you haven't a garden, create your Moon garden in a large pot, which can be moved about to catch the moonlight.

Choose silvery plants such as Lavenders, silvery Thymes, Sages and plants that have white flowers that will glow in the moonlight. Bring in a bowl for Water, add crystals and include a mirror.

Willow

Salix

'Tree of inspiration and intuition'

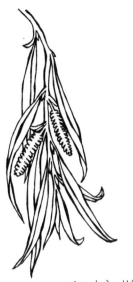

Willow is a native of Britain and is found throughout low-lying regions, where the roots help to bind the soil along the riverbanks. If they are not pollarded (cut to head height, out of the reach of grazing animals), Willows grow into large trees, their branches often leaning right out into the Water.

Willow is the 4th tree in the Celtic Tree Ogham, representing the unconscious, the intuition, inspired actions, fertility, vision, dreams and expressed emotions. Its ruling planet is the Moon.

There are 19 species of Willow native to Britain and many more are bred by nurseries to produce ornamental trees, such as the weeping Willow, the twisted Willow and the many Willows with the brightly coloured bark used in fancy basket making. All the different Willows have similar properties.

Growing Willow Trees

All Willows are fast-growing and easy to grow from cuttings rather than from seed (*see Elder, page 46*). The Willow is so vigorous that twigs can be planted directly into the soil and they will quickly put down roots if kept damp. They can be planted to create fast-growing living screens or living Willow domes or dens.

In the garden Willow can be coppiced to keep it a small shrub. Cut it back to ground level in the Spring, after enjoying the brightly coloured twigs in the Winter months. Regular cutting back will ensure a plentiful supply of flexible rods for use in the garden, for weaving and for many other creative crafts.

Folklore and Legend

Willow is sacred to Imbolc, bringing movement, a quickening of the life force and power from within. In European mythology it symbolizes death of the old and is seen as a force for change and new growth, as it brings a release of energy.

Willow has always been known as a tree of enchantment and has been used for charms of Love and binding. Long thin Willow whips can be used to bind charms together, adding the fertile potency of the Willow.

In the past Willow was said to bring good luck in childbirth and was considered to be a female energy, sacred to the Moon and our Watery emotional natures. It was also sacred to Spring maiden goddesses such as Brigit, Bride, Brigantia, Gwenhyver, Cordelia and Blodeuwedd. In Celtic legend the willowy Spring maiden initiated the young king of the new year and prepared the way for fertility and new growth.

Deserted lovers would wear green Willow to help them to express their emotions and share their heartache with others.

Willow wands were used to invoke the Muses, bring vivid dreams and facilitate the release of emotions.

The Wisdom of Willow

Willow is a Water-seeking tree, linked to the female rhythms, the pull of the Moon, the power of the unconscious, intuition, dreams and visions. It helps us to keep in touch with these deep parts of ourselves and to bring them out into the open.

Similarly, Willow helps us to contact our emotions and act on them. Emotional stagnation and unhappiness can lead to illness, but Willow will help us to move through the different layers of our sadness and gain inner strength and healing from the experience.

Willow twigs are very flexible, teaching us to move with life rather than resist what we are feeling. When one of its branches becomes disconnected, it will grow into a new tree if it finds soil, teaching us that contained within a loss there is always a new direction and the capacity for new growth and healing.

Willow reminds us to make the most of the potential inherent in every situation, to act on our intuition and to move with change.

The Wood and Its Uses

Willow has a pale fine-textured soft wood. It is light and tough, but perishes easily in damp conditions. It is used to make cricket bats, as it can absorb energy without splintering. Harp soundboxes were originally carved from solid pieces of Willow because it could take the tension of the strings whilst remaining vibrant.

Willows are traditionally pollarded or coppiced to give a regular crop of small poles and whips suitable for fencing, basketry and firewood.

Willow whips and withies can be cut and used any time, although they are best cut between November and March, when they are not in leaf. Bundle them together and leave them under a North-facing hedge, where they will remain pliant for a few months, provided they do not dry out. Freshly cut Willow is called 'green Willow' and can be used for weaving and binding.

Basket-maker's Willow is specially prepared and can be soaked in a bath of Water to revive its pliancy at any time. Any basket-maker's Willow that is not used can be dried out again and used another time, but you cannot do this with freshly cut Willow.

The traditional besom broom has a shaft of Willow and the Birch twigs of the brush end are bound with Willow whips.

The roots of the Crack Willow can be boiled to obtain a purple dye traditionally used to decorate eggs at Easter/Spring Equinox.

Willow wands and talismans are used for moving energy along, for releasing the intuition, connecting to dreams, obtaining guidance from the Otherworld and for any work with the Moon.

Herbal Uses: *Salix*

Bark

Willow bark is an old remedy for rheumatism, arthritis, muscle aches and stiffness and all diseases caused by damp conditions. It contains salicylic acid, the basis of aspirin, and can be used to relieve pain. Collect the bark in the Springtime, being careful to only take patches (see page 17). Make into a decoction or a poultice (see page 35).

The bark and catkins can be used as an anti-aphrodisiac, a sexual sedative, to lessen sexual desire.

Leaves

Young Willow leaves can be chewed to help bleeding gums and mouth ulcers. An infusion (see page 35) of the leaves is a good gargle for sore throats and can be taken for colds and 'flu and to bring down a fever. It will help eliminate toxins from the body through the urinary system and can be drunk as a tonic after illness.

Willow Flower Remedy

This is taken to help clear discontentment and old patterns of resentment that may be smouldering beneath the surface. It is good for shifting a negative outlook and will assist in the release of emotional pain by facilitating the expression of feelings through crying and allowing suppressed sadness to come to the surface.

Healing Properties

If there has been a crisis or loss, sometimes an emotional numbness sets in because the feelings are too painful. Willow teaches us that these feelings must be felt so that they can come to the surface and be released. By releasing this emotional congestion, it lifts the spirits and, when relevant, can bring the recognition that we are not victims, that we are all responsible for our own destiny.

Willow can also help us to let go of conditioned responses to life's experiences and to seek acceptance of ourselves and others through Unconditional Love. It helps us to remember to flow with the healing process and to be open to what lessons we can learn from it so that we can move on.

Willow also enables us to act on our inspired leaps of intuition, to have the confidence to go forward into the unknown without fear. This is the essential key of Willow: to trust our intuition and to act on it immediately.

Willow is also the tree of dreaming. When we dream, we tap in to our imagination, our longings, our deepest thoughts and feelings and release our unconscious. If you lose touch with your dreams, sleep with a Willow wand under your pillow and spend time with Willow trees.

Spirit of Willow

Spring Equinox

'Festival of Balance and Potential'

20–23 March in the Northern Hemisphere

20–23 September in the Southern Hemisphere

Spring Equinox is celebrated as the first day of Spring, when day and night are equal in both hemispheres. All of Nature is stirring now and showing signs of activity after the Winter sleep. Buds are bursting on the trees, Spring flowers are coming out and seeds are germinating.

The power of the Sun is increasing, the days are lengthening and the nights are shortening. We begin to feel empowered to reach out for what we want and to take risks, strike out on our own, go for walks and connect to the Earth again.

We can use the potential and fertility of this time to create opportunities for positive change in our lives and in the world. At this point we are poised between opposite forces, light and dark, receptive and active, unconscious and conscious, inner and outer. These can be united within us so that we are whole and balanced individuals. This gives birth to actions that come from the heart.

In the past the fertile Earth goddess Eostre was honoured at this time in celebration of new life and gestation. Dragon processions celebrated the emerging active energy of the Earth and eggs were used as a potent symbol of new life and rebirth.

Spring Equinox Celebration

- Θ This is a day to be outside, to enjoy the elements, to run wild like a March Hare, to experience the awakening energy of the Earth.
- Θ Meet for a shared breakfast or arrange a meeting place for a shared walk that will take you out into an open space, such as a

common, moor or hilltop. Ask everyone to bring a decorated hard-boiled egg, picnic food and drink to share and something to fly in the wind such as kites, ribbons or prayer flags.

⊖ Before you begin your walk, gather in a circle and if there are some new faces, welcome them and help them to feel included. Everyone in turn says their name and as they do so, each person places their egg at the centre of the circle and makes a 'pledge of potential' to help the Earth in some way. Inspire each other with your boldness and creative plans! Enjoy the sight of all the eggs lying in the grass and pass around a hot fruit cup, offering a toast to everyone's endeavours as you take a sip.

⊖ Gather up the eggs (eat en route!) and use the walk to network and develop the ideas and plans put forward.

⊖ At the top of the hill or wherever you decide to stop, fly kites and plant the prayer flags in the Earth, sending out messages of hope and prayers for peace on the wind. You can make these beforehand or provide materials for making them on the day. Take some pens and write prayers, messages of hope and good wishes onto ribbons. These can be tied onto a stick and run with in the wind.

⊖ Have a shared picnic and take bags to clear up any rubbish you find, especially plastic, which can blow far in the strong March winds.

A chant:

> 'Building bridges between our divisions,
> I reach out to you as you reach out to me.
> With all of our voices and all of our visions,
> Together we can make such a sweet harmony.
> Together we can make such a sweet harmony.'

Spring Equinox Ceremony

Θ Create a central indoor shrine with green and yellow cloths and place a basket of (fairly traded) chocolate eggs at the centre. Add vases of Spring flowers and a circle of nightlights in bowls of sand.

Θ Begin by singing the chant and circling round this central shrine, using staffs or walking sticks as a way to create rhythm. Build up the energy as you welcome the active forces of the Earth and celebrate the awakening Earth dragon. Call out all that you welcome into your life. Let your imagination run wild! Release and energize!

Θ Welcome each element by singing each one into the circle. Be spontaneous, using words and sounds that help you make a connection. Echo each other's words and sounds, build and develop them so that all the sounds gather momentum and flow together.

Θ Let the sounds gradually fade away and stand in the stillness for a while. Meditate together on the potential of Spring and on any projects or plans you are giving birth to.

Θ When you feel ready, call upon the energy of the Equinox Hare to lead you on a journey within, asking for inspiration and wisdom for your new plans. Remain standing with your staff or walking stick and sing sounds and notes to facilitate your journey with Hare. Picture yourself going down through a hole in the Earth and down a tunnel. Where this leads to is your own personal inner journey. Keep your quest for wisdom and inspiration as your strongly held intention as you follow the Hare and sing your connection to Dreamtime.

Θ When you feel your journey is done, return to your tunnel and wait, gently toning one long single note on each outbreath until everyone is doing the same.

Θ If you are a small group, take it in turns to speak or sing your journey from this place between the worlds. Do not try to interpret it at this point.

Θ When everyone has recounted their journey, thank the Hare and sing yourselves fully back.

Θ Each person takes a chocolate egg from the centre and names the project, plans or changes they are giving birth to. Take in the Spirit of potential as you eat your egg!

Θ Close the circle by singing out the elements as you sung them in.

Θ Bless the food and drink and as you eat, share the insights and understanding you gained on your journey and your plans for the Spring and Summer months.

Winds of Change

At this time of year we can inspire each other with prophecies of hope, the power of 'We' and our willingness and power to bring change into the world as we create opportunities for a bright new future.

Inspire others to join in and spread actions with heart, actions that bring heartfelt common bonds of friendship and community into our lives! Bring the Equinox spark of fertility to your most positive actions! Feel the winds of change and the potential we are part of vibrating in every cell in your body!

Green Guerrillas

In the 1970s a band of artists in New York set out to plant flowers in the city. They planted up traffic islands and bombarded derelict sites with seed bombs – balloons filled with seeds, soil and Water. The city authorities began to notice improvements and eventually grants were made available to develop hundreds of community gardens, transforming the city and making it a better place in which to live and work. A strong sense of community and neighbourliness began to flourish as people came and shared in Nature together.

Look around your local community for areas you can transform with flowers this year. Now is the time for dividing plants and digging up self-seeded plants. Find homes for these, replanting them into the community. Pot them up and give them away rather than discard them and share the seedlings you grow. Sharing plants is a way of reaching out to people who share a common interest and a way of getting to know new people.

Our communities may encourage or dampen our positivity and creativity. Either way, our own actions can have a knock-on effect, so do something that inspires others and make a difference on your own doorstep! If your house is straight out onto the street, fill a planter with bright flowers and put it outside your door. In a busy street it may be a good idea to fix a wooden planter to the wall with brackets. Before long others will do the same and the street will be transformed!

Herb Spiral

Choose three edible herbs that you are drawn towards and begin to grow them from organic seed on your window ledges now. Learn about their herbal and energetic properties and on fine sunny days begin making your herb spiral.

Mark out a circle by putting a stake at the centre, putting a loop of string over it and following it round, marking the edge with stones. Its size depends on how much space you have available. Lay down several layers of cardboard and pile the soil, mixed with compost, into a heap on top of this, using stones or upturned bottles to mark out a spiral.

Plant your herbs out when ready (or alternatively buy small ready-grown plants) and use them for herb teas, in salads, in your cooking, for medicine and for healing. Thank them when you pick them and build up a relationship with them and a working knowledge of their uses.

Well Dressings

Well dressings are pictures made out of flowers, petals, leaves, seeds, bark, moss and other natural materials, which are pressed into wet clay on a board. Making the board is the first step and it must be made of natural wood. Floorboarding slotted together with a brace across the back works well. Cover the whole thing with raised headless nails such as panel pins; this helps the clay to cling to the board.

The board must be soaked in Water for 24 hours before the clay is spread on. A smooth consistency of clay is important. Water is added and it is traditionally trodden with the feet until it is the consistency of soft butter.

A design can be worked out and then drawn out on paper the size of the board. This is then laid over the spread clay and pricked through with a sharp point. Remove the paper and define the outline of the prick marks, traditionally with the small dark cones from the Alder tree.

The picture is then filled in using a variety of natural materials. Work from the bottom upward, with the petals and leaves overlapping each other to allow the rain to run off. The wet clay keeps everything fresh and the picture lasts for a week or so, depending on the weather and the materials used.

Having survived in Derbyshire under the wing of the church, this ancient tradition is being revived in other parts of Britain as once again the Spirit of Water is being honoured.

Alder

Alnus glutinosa

'Tree of balance and inspired action'

Native to Britain and Europe, the Alder is mostly found growing along riverbanks and streams and in swampy ground. The roots help to fix nitrogen in the soil and the many tiny rootlets help to hold the soil of riverbanks together.

Alder is the 3rd tree in the Celtic Tree Ogham, representing a balanced perspective, preservation, protection, challenge, discrimination and firm foundations.

It is associated with Pisces, the bringing of inner vision and inspiration, and also Venus, the Moon and Mars.

Alder is most easily recognized by its red catkins in the early Spring, which give the whole tree a red haze. At this time of year it is possible to see the new male and female catkins, new leafbuds and the cones of last year's fruit on a single tree.

Alder is the only broadleaved tree to produce cones, which grow in clusters of twos and threes. They are small and green at first, turning black once the seeds are shed. The seeds provide valuable Winter food for birds.

Growing Alder Trees

Alder cones can be collected when green, before they open. Dry them in brown paper bags and they will open to release small winged seeds which can be sown immediately. Cover them with a thin layer of sharp sand and leave over Winter to germinate the following Spring. Alder can be planted to enrich poor ground and to prevent soil erosion along the riverbanks.

Folklore and Legend

In Irish legend, the first male was created from Alder and the first female from Rowan. Alder was known as King Alder or the Elf King throughout Europe. Alder's name derives from the Old English *ealdor*, meaning 'chief', and relates to the office of alderman, a senior member of a Welsh or English local council previously elected by fellow members and considered to be a special honour.

Traditionally, the Alder was the haunt of faeries and was associated with protecting the faerie realms. Water spirits or undines are said to protect this tree and it is also linked to unicorns.

In Celtic mythology the Alder is associated with courage and enthusiasm for a fight. In the past, a red dye obtained from the Alder was used to stain the skin before going into battle. In Welsh legend the Alder is associated with Bran the Blessed, a mighty giant and Celtic king who brought protection, resurrection, healing and oracular knowledge.

Alder is a tree of balance, associated with both Water and Fire. It has a dynamic Fiery energy, while its roots are deep in Water, providing intuition and inspiration from within.

Alder whistles were used to whistle up Nature spirits and to conjure the Spirit of Air and the winds.

The buds of the Alder are set in spirals, which are a powerful symbol of everlasting life and resurrection.

When Alder is cut, the wood turns red, as if it were bleeding, and this has helped to protect the Alder from being cut down.

The black Alder cones are traditionally used in the well-dressing pictures of Derbyshire (*see page 195*). They are known as 'black knobs' and are pressed into the clay to help define the picture.

The Wisdom of Alder

Alder has always been associated with Fire, through its red dye, its red catkins and its ability to resist rotting in Water. It is also associated with Water, with the Otherworld, the world of the faeries and life outside our safe surface reality. It brings balance between the inner and the outer worlds, between our intuitive receptive selves and our rational logical selves. It helps us to harness discrimination as we find our way through life's challenges. If we approach our problems using both our intuitive and our rational minds, we will be more stable and have a secure foundation from which to move forward.

Alder helps us to see beyond the obvious. It helps us to work with the traditions and knowledge of the past and to follow our instincts to free these understandings from deep inside ourselves. In this way we become aware of what is going on below the surface as well as on the physical levels.

The Wood and Its Uses

Alder wood is red when cut, yellow when seasoned, oily and water-resistant. It is very durable for all outdoor and Winter use, becoming hard and black when immersed in water.

In the past Alder was used extensively for the foundations of bridges and for the poles on which swamp and lakeside houses were built to keep them raised above the water. It was also used for boats, water pumps, troughs, sluices, water barrels, milk pails, weather boards, clogs, the soles of shoes and cart wheels.

In Scotland it was used for making chairs and was once known as 'Scottish mahogany'. The roots and knots in the wood were used as decoration in cabinet making. Alder polishes up well and takes a good finish.

Fresh Alder wood was brought into the house in the Spring to catch woodworm. When the beetle hatched out, it laid its eggs in the Alder, which could then be burnt. The sticky Spring leaves were strewn over floors or hung up to catch insects such as fleas, and then these too could be burnt when the insects had become stuck.

Alder produces a hot charcoal, used by the smiths of the past for making weapons. These were traditionally made in the Spring, ready for the new hunting season.

Alder is easy to work and is good for carving. An Alder wand, touchwood or talisman will help to balance intuition with willpower, receptivity with action. Magical panpipes can be made by cutting a variety of lengths of Alder and loosening the bark by gently tapping the wood. Within a short while the inner wood dries and shrinks and can gently be eased out from the bark. The bark tubes can be bound together side by side and played by blowing across their tops to get a variety of 'windy' notes.

Herbal Uses: *Alnus glutinosa*

Leaves

These are cooling and soothing and can be mashed up with a little warm milk or water to make a poultice to reduce swellings. Bind the mash over the place needing treatment with fresh Alder leaves.

Use the fresh leaves inside your boots or shoes to soothe aching or burning feet or to enable you to travel long distances and keep your feet cool.

Bark

The bark has a similar action to the leaves and can be made into a decoction (see page 35). This can also be used for burns and inflammations. Soak a cotton cloth in the mixture to bathe the skin and drink the herbal remedy.

The bark yields a powerful red dye greatly favoured by the Celts. If copper is added to the dye bath, the colour turns black.

Flowers

These make a beautiful green dye associated with the clothes of faeries and outlaws. These green clothes were adopted not only for camouflage but also to enlist the energy and the protection of the Alder trees.

Twigs

These make a brown dye. If mixed with the young shoots in March they make a golden orange dye.

Healing Properties

Meditating with the Alder brings a balanced outlook and provides a firm foundation for blending our Watery intuitive selves with our outer Fiery selves. Their combined strength will help us to deal with any of life's challenges.

The strength of Alder lies in its ability to help us to face things that have previously been hidden below the surface. If we have the courage, these can be brought out into the open, challenged and lovingly dealt with.

Alder brings healing to the heart and emotions and helps us to bring Spirit into our actions.

Spirit of
Alder

Beltain

'Festival of Fertility and Union'

End of April/beginning of May in the Northern Hemisphere

End of October/beginning of November in the Southern Hemisphere

Beltain is a celebration of the potency of the Earth and the forces of Nature. This is the beginning of the most active part of the year and the beginning of Summer. All of life is bursting with fertility, sap is rising, birdsong fills the air and growth is everywhere.

The Earth becomes clothed in green, personified in the past as the Green Goddess and the Green Man. Beltain is a celebration of sexuality and the fertility that springs from the union of female and male forces. It is a time for practising the art of wooing, for letting passions fly in the exuberant joy of the moment. It is a time to express yourself, but also to remember to stay grounded.

Ask yourself what you wish to give energy to. Where will you put your focus? What can you change for the better? What actions can you make that will help the spread of goodwill and Love in the world? All too soon this highly fertile time will be spent, so make the most of its raw energy for initiating plans and visions. Everything you do now will bring you closer to your goals, as the expansive energy of the moment carries you along.

The boundaries between our world and the world of Spirit are thin at this time (as at Samhain), especially at dawn and dusk, and we can become 'spell-bound' by the moment, spinning off into Dreamtime.

Traditionally, this is a time for staying up all night, for sleeping out on the Earth, especially at springs and wells, for jumping the Beltain Fire, for dancing around the maypole and for walking spirals and labyrinths. Beltain is a festival for celebrating our friends and lovers, and the potency of union of all kinds.

Beltain Celebration

- ◎ If possible, celebrate Beltain Eve when the Moon is full or waxing to full and be outside all night. Watch the Sun rise and experience being outside at dawn.

- ◎ Arrange a place to gather in a garden or on someone's land where it is possible to have a fire. Bring tents, sleeping bags, blankets and water-proof sheets so that the children can go to sleep when they are ready.

- ◎ Bring food and drink to share, firewood for the fire, and dress as the Spirit of the Green Man or Green Goddess. Bring whistles and drums and use them to conjure up the Spirit of the Greenwood and to facilitate dancing. This is traditionally a time for interweaving dances around a maypole or a tree. Find someone who can teach these or make up your own. Use music and dance to bring people together in celebration of life and each other.

- ◎ Create a special moment to jump the Beltain Fire, leaving behind what is holding you back and calling out as you jump: 'I leave behind…'

- ◎ Partners and lovers, parents and children and close friends can hold hands and jump together, pledging themselves to each other, to joint projects and to ways forward. Call out as you jump: 'I pledge myself to…'

A chant:

'Round and round we go.
We hold each other's hands
And live our lives in a circle.
Our Love is strong
And the dance goes on.'

Beltain Ceremony

⊚ Decorate the base of a tree with flowers and place a basket of cut ribbons beneath it.

⊚ Gather around the tree. Build up the energy of a chant, dance and hold hands, welcoming contact with the Dryad of the tree.

⊚ Share a grounding exercise, breathing deeply down into your belly and letting your energy drop down your legs into the Earth. Feel yourself anchored and held stable by your roots as you continue to travel down into the Earth until you reach the living core of Fire at the centre. Draw this limitless fertile power up through your roots and into your body. Feel it bringing you renewed energy.

⊚ Open the circle by welcoming the Spirit of each element using words and sounds and making heartfelt connections, so that you really feel what gifts each element brings to you at this time. Bring this awareness out into the circle: 'I thank [name the element] for its gift of...' so that each person conjures up their own links of gratitude and connection.

⊚ To the sound of whistles or drums, let each person dance towards the tree, expressing their most beautiful self and deepest connection to the tree and the Earth.

⊚ Take a piece of ribbon from the basket and tie it to the tree as you give your personal pledge to bring two parts of your life together that need to be joined and healed. Dance back out when you feel ready.

⊚ When everyone in the circle has made their dance and pledge, hold hands and spiral in to stand around the tree decked with pledge ribbons. Send your pledges on their way by letting out a long note on each outbreath, bathing each other and the tree in sound. This works best if it lasts for at least five minutes, so that the very air is vibrating with harmonizing sound.

◎ In the silence that follows, send your Love and goodwill out into the world, to those you Love and to those in power, whose change of heart could bring peaceful unions and world harmony.

◎ Close the circle by thanking the elements for their part in the growing season and the tree for being part of your ceremony. Spiral out, dancing and expressing your exuberance and Love for life. The ribbons can be left on the tree or taken with you to remind you of your pledge.

Spirals and Labyrinths

At this time of year the potent energy of the Earth can be harnessed or improved by creating stone spirals or labyrinths. The energy they create spreads out from the centre in ever-widening circles. They can be used to activate the land and unblock stagnant Earth energies. They can be walked or danced or used for meditation and transformation. *(See Spiral Dance, page 177)*

A temporary spiral or labyrinth, indoors or out, can be made out of bark mulch, potting compost, free-flowing cooking salt, powdered chalk or sand.

Making a Spiral

1. Begin by deciding on the size of the circular space the spiral will occupy. The size of the spiral itself depends on the space and materials available. Stone is the most permanent form of material. Stones can be interspersed with herbs such as Thyme or Lavender or you

can use gravel, make a mosaic spiral or cut one out of the turf.

2. Place a stone where you think the centre should be and with a piece of string held at the centre, mark out the central circle, placing small stones as markers and leaving an opening on one side. A six-and-a-half feet (two metre) central circle will leave plenty of room for movement and turning round.

3. Curve your spiral clockwise out from the central circle, keeping an even pathway by using a stick the width of the path.

4. Place a flat stone at the centre where you can sit in contemplation or place things.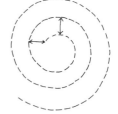

A Labyrinth

A labyrinth is one continuous path which takes you to the centre and out again. It may twist and turn, but as long as you keep walking forwards you will always come out again. There are many different designs, but a true labyrinth will always follow this same basic principle.

Labyrinths are used for meditation, initiation, for taking a question to the centre and bringing an answer out, for finding inner clarity or leaving behind and transforming an old part of yourself. Labyrinths can also be used for a rite of passage, which always consists of three phases:

Going into the centre: *Making a separation from the old.*

At the centre: *Marking the transition by a symbolic gesture or action.*

Coming out from the centre: *Affirming and integrating the changed and new.*

Making a Labyrinth

Follow the pattern to create a small labyrinth.

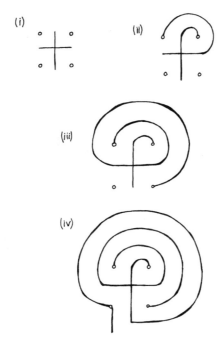

Build spirals or labyrinths out in the wild, in the woods or on a beach. Make them large or small, depending on the materials available. Create them out of stones, shells, twigs, grasses and flowers. Walk them, dance them, energize yourself with their special energy.

The larger classical seven-coil is good for a permanent site.

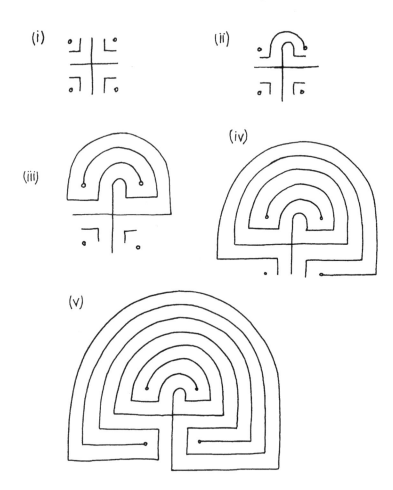

Making Flower Remedies

This is the beginning of the season when most plants and trees come into flower and these can be made into flower remedies.

The most famous flower remedies are those pioneered by the Welsh-born Dr Edward Bach in the early 1900s. He began a system of curing illness by focusing not on the illness itself but on the underlying cause of the illness: the mental and emotional state of the patient. When he died in 1936, he believed his system of 38 flower remedies, covering 38 states of mind, to be complete. He grouped them under seven headings:

For fear: Rock Rose, Mimulus, Cherry Plum, Aspen, Red Chestnut

For uncertainty: Cerato, Scleranthus, Gentian, Gorse, Hornbeam, Wild Oat

For insufficient interest in present circumstances: Clematis, Honeysuckle, Wild Rose, Olive, White Chestnut, Chestnut Bud

For loneliness: Water Violet, Impatiens, Heather

For being oversensitive to influences and ideas: Agrimony, Centuary, Walnut, Holly

For despondency or despair: Larch, Pine, Elm, Sweet Chestnut, Star of Bethlehem, Willow, Oak, Crab Apple

For overcare for the welfare of others: Chicory, Vervain, Vine, Beech, Rock Water

Dr Bach freely published his findings so that they were available for everyone to use, 'with only a little knowledge, sympathy and an understanding of human nature'.

Each of the plants has its own unique level of action and can be worked with intuitively or according to any of the books on the Bach flower remedies. Remedies can be combined in twos and threes where more than one issue needs to be addressed.

The flower remedies are simple to make and use.

1. Begin by sitting near the plant you are drawn towards. Ground yourself and connect to the plant in meditation.

2. Take some spring water and thank it, bless it and ask it to store the energy of the flowers.

3. On a sunny day, gently cut the flowers, letting them fall face down into a glass dish of natural spring water. Use a stalk or leaf from the same plant to turn them over if necessary.

4. Leave the bowl next to the plant or tree and let it stand in the sunlight for at least three hours, raising it up on a stone if necessary.

5. Scoop off the petals with a stalk or leaf from the same plant and mix the infused Water with an equal amount of brandy to preserve it.

6. Pour it into a clean bottle and place it for a while amongst the plants you have used. This is the 'mother tincture', the essence of the plant.

7. Make this into the 'stock essence' by adding seven drops to a clean 10ml bottle containing half spring water and half brandy.

8. Using your stock essence, take four drops in a little spring water three times a day.

Besides the listed remedies of Dr Bach, flowers from other trees and plants can be made into flower remedies in the same way, especially if you are drawn to work with them and their healing properties.

When you begin taking a remedy, observe yourself and any subtle changes that may occur over a period of several weeks. Keep notes and follow your intuitive impressions of how the plant may be working with you on emotional, mental and spiritual levels.

Hawthorn

Crataegus monogyna

'Tree of the heart'

This fast-growing tree is found throughout Britain, all over Europe, Western Asia and North Africa and has been used for centuries as a hedging plant to mark field boundaries. It can be cut back and laid and makes an impenetrable barrier. Birds and small mammals find nesting places and food within the shelter of the thorny twigs.

Hawthorn is the 6th tree of the Celtic Tree Ogham, representing Love, fertility, the heart, protection, the release of blocked energy and preparation for spiritual growth. It is associated with Thor and Jupiter, gods of fertility and good fortune.

Ideal for the garden, Hawthorn can be used for a hedge or left to grow into a small tree. It is a long-lived tree, living for 400 years if the conditions are favourable. Often you can find clumps of twisted old trees, which may be marking places of important Earth energy or the site of an old Druid grove.

Hawthorn is often found growing in towns, in the remnants of old hedgerows or green lanes. It still seems to retain the Spirit of the wild places and holds a special place in our affections, especially the May blossom, which turns the hedgerows white and fills the Air with its heady scent.

Hawthorn is also known as Whitethorn, Quickthorn, Hagthorn, Haegthorn, Thorn or the May.

Growing Hawthorn Trees

The fleshy red berries, called haws, contain a single seed, which should be stratified (see Rowan, page 73). The seeds may take two Winters to germinate.

Folklore and Legend

Hawthorn folk customs go back to the time when the Earth was seen as the potent life force and its fertility was revered and celebrated, especially at Beltain. The May Queen was the Green Goddess who joined with her consort the Green Man, Jack of the Green, Jack in the May or the May King, and their union blessed the fertility of the land.

Beltain Eve was a night for revelry and the greenwood marriage, when couples re-enacted the joining of god and goddess to bring fertility to the land. These Spring rites later became outlawed by the church, which tried to re-establish them as May Day celebrations with a virginal May Queen. All the previous folk customs of the Hawthorn were reversed and discredited. Despite this, many of the old customs lived on. Marriages took place at this time and the bride and groom would carry or wear May blossom. Garlands of Mayflowers would be hung around their bed for fertility and lasting Love.

After the calendar changes in 1752 the May tree was seldom in blossom by the beginning of May but Hawthorn and May blossom continued to be powerful symbols of sexuality and union of all kinds.

The popular rhyme 'Here we go gathering nuts in May' was more likely to be 'knots of May' in its original form. May is the wrong month for nuts and the rhyme would have referred to the knots of May gathered to deck the maypole and hang on doors for good luck and fertility.

Hawthorn was also used for protection. Sprigs were hung in the cradles of newborn babies as protection from harm. Twigs were woven into globes and circles and used as protective charms. Fire charms were made to protect the house and hearth. A twig of Oak, Ash and Hawthorn bound together with red ribbon was also a protective charm.

The maypole was originally a living Hawthorn tree brought into the village with its resident Dryad. It was danced around and celebrated as a potent and fertile life force and the Tree Spirit's help would have been enlisted to bless the fertility of the land.

Solitary Hawthorns often marked old sacred groves or meeting places, wells, springs, underground Water and faerie trysting places. Groups of old Hawthorn trees, especially if they grew in threes, were considered to be potent places and were treated with great respect. Oak, Ash and Hawthorn growing together was also considered a potent combination, as was Hawthorn and Elder.

Hawthorns were said to guard the entrances to the world of the faerie. Hawthorns growing on a hill were said to mark the faerie hills. Sitting under Hawthorns on a Beltain Eve, and any time between then and Midsummer, was said to result in enchantment or being fetched away by the faeries.

A Hawthorn brooch or 'Albion knot' was used to demonstrate allegiance to the fair folk and the Spirit of Nature.

Any lone Hawthorn was held in so much respect that paths and roads were redirected round it and proposed buildings were re-sited to avoid cutting it down, as such Hawthorns were said to mark the faerie paths that were never to be blocked or interfered with.

Hawthorn trees next to wells or springs were decorated in the Spring and hung with ribbons and wish rags. These were tied to the tree to attract Love and healing, and gifts were left for the faeries and the Earth spirits protected by the tree.

The Wisdom of Hawthorn

If you wish to learn from the wisdom of this powerful tree then choose an old tree or a group of trees and spend time sitting with them. Hang a ribbon in the tree as you offer your allegiance to the Earth.

Hawthorn helps us to slip into a meditative heart-centred place, so that we can make a loving response to any emotional difficulties we may be experiencing. It is a potent giver of life-enhancing energy that will help us to move into a more open-hearted spirituality based on Unconditional Love. Here at the beginning of the new Aquarian Age, with all of its possibilities and potential, Hawthorn helps us to transform our actions from taking to giving. We begin to act from our hearts, healing the hurts of generations, opening to the flow of Love as a powerful force that can transform our lives and our world.

The Wood and Its Uses

Hawthorn is a hard dense wood. It is a beautiful orange colour, sands well and polishes up to a good finish, but it cracks easily when drying and has an irregular grain.

As Hawthorn is under the protection of the faerie folk, it was considered bad luck to cut the tree down and consequently the wood had few uses. It was used for engravers' blocks, however, and the roots were prized for combs and small boxes. It was considered lucky to use for handles, charms, brooches and talismans. 'Albion knots' were pinned to the clothing to bring good fortune, protection, allegiance to the Earth and the faerie realms.

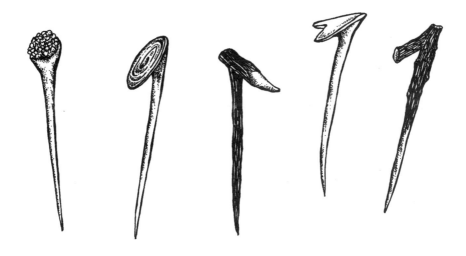

Albion Knots

Give Hawthorn as a gift of Love and healing. To find Hawthorn wood to use, keep your eyes open for hedge layers as they cut back the hedges or use your own hedge trimmings.

For wand making, it is better to go to the tree and ask for a wand, following your intuition at all times. Hawthorn makes a good ceremonial wand, bringing a deep connection to Unconditional Love. Small healing wands can be used to reinforce the path of the heart, to energize all acts of Love and to invoke the power of the fertile life force.

Herbal and Edible Uses: *Crataegus monogyna*

Hawthorn is the prime remedy for the heart and the circulation and is both recommended and safe to take over long periods, especially during old age.

The flowers, leaves and berries can all be used as a safe heart tonic, to open the arteries and to improve the circulation and blood supply to all body tissues.

Hawthorn is helpful for high blood pressure, hardening of the arteries, heart palpitations and all heart conditions.

The leaves, flowers and berries also have a beneficial effect on the nervous system, relieving stress and anxiety. They bring calm sleep if drunk at night.

Young Leaves and Leafbuds

These are known as 'bread and cheese' and can be nibbled straight from the tree, added to salads and dried for herb tea.

Flowers

The flowers or flowerbuds can be eaten or made into tea for a daily tonic. Add them to salads and fruit salads. They can also be made into wine and syrups.

Berries

The bright red clusters of fruit are called haws, pixie pears, cuckoo breads and chucky cheese. These can be gathered in Autumn before the leaves fall, dried in brown paper bags and made into a decoction (*see page 35*) whenever needed. They can also be made into wine.

Haw Brandy

This is a delicious drink made the same way as sloe gin but using haws and brandy instead (*see Blackthorn, page 273, for method*).

Hawthorn Flower Remedy

This is not one of Dr Bach's remedies but can easily be made at this time of year. It helps to ease emotional extremes and is used for healing broken hearts and to release anger, disappointment and bitterness after failed Love.

It also helps heal the inner child by helping to resolve with Unconditional Love any areas that might manifest as a victim complex, keeping you vulnerable and lacking in power and energy. Use it wherever there is difficulty with giving or receiving Unconditional Love.

Healing Properties

Emotional extremes sap energy from the body, creating physical problems brought on by stress, distress and inner turmoil. Hawthorn will help to restore a calm outlook. It helps us to trust and let go of fear. It releases blocked energy, brings transformation and movement, and helps us to move through emotional levels, from the surface layers to deeper levels, to the roots of our problems and illnesses. We eventually come to the awareness that Love is the greatest healer and from this inspiration we can begin a new journey.

Any act of Love is an act of power. We understand at a deeper level that the Love we send out comes back to us and we become open to the creative flow of Love, through which we are able to heal ourselves. From here we can take responsibility for our own illnesses and our own paths of healing.

Spirit of
Hawthorn

Summer Solstice

'Festival of Achievement'

20–23 June in the Northern Hemisphere

20–23 December in the Southern Hemisphere

This is Summer's height, Midsummer, the longest day and the shortest night of the Earth's solar year. Here we celebrate the completion of the cycle that began at the Winter Solstice.

Solstice means 'standing of the Sun' and we can connect to this great turning point in the Earth's yearly cycle by taking a moment to stop, be still and look back at our own unique journey since the Winter Solstice. By celebrating our achievements and acknowledging our failures, we can make sense of our actions and understand what can be learned from them.

From now to the Winter Solstice everything on the Earth will be withdrawing within. We can use this time to focus on what we wish to nurture and develop in ourselves during the coming months.

In the past the Summer Solstice was an important occasion. People stayed up all night to watch the Sun come up at dawn. Many of the stone circles in the Northern Hemisphere are aligned to the Solstice sunrise. Midsummer's Eve and Midsummer's Day were traditionally the time for carnivals, processions and circular walks.

Summer Solstice is a time to count our blessings, to celebrate our achievements and our expansive, expressive selves. It is a time to celebrate each other, to pass on the Spirit of generosity and goodwill in ever-widening circles of positive energy.

Summer Solstice Celebration

☼ The Summer Solstice is the moment to celebrate ourselves as individuals within our community. Organize a procession on Midsummer's Eve, letting friends and family know a gathering place and time. Ask everyone to bring a picnic and to dress bold and beautiful!

☼ Plan a circular walk to a picnic spot where you can have a fire in the evening. Encourage a carnival atmosphere, with a planned theme to facilitate dressing up, puppets, decorated hats, plays, banners and flags. Ask musicians to come and play and ask everyone to bring drums and percussion. Encourage personal expression and creativity in all aspects of the event.

☼ Stay up all night and climb to a high place just before dawn to watch the Solstice sunrise or gather at a local power spot or stone circle. If you are on the East coast, watch the Sun rise over the sea.

☼ As the Sun comes over the horizon, become aware of your feet on the Earth and the pulse of her energy. Commit yourself to help her in some way. This may not be clear as yet, but your heartfelt intent will open the possibilities for this to happen.

☼ The Summer Solstice is a doorway into the second half of the year, energizing the paths that lead within. Stand on the threshold and ask yourself what you wish to encourage in your life.

A chant:

> 'Many thousand years we have come
> To be here in this moment with you,
> Earth, the Moon, the stars and the Sun,
> Dancing the dream awake.'

Solstice Ceremony

- ☀ Before the ceremony, create a ring of stones or crystals as a central focus and ask everyone to find five stones, one to represent each element, and to bring them to the ceremony.

  Begin with a shared grounding exercise that helps everyone to feel connected to the Earth. If it is dry, lie down on the Earth and feel the pulse of her living energy beneath you.

- ☀ Open the circle by creating a cairn of elemental blessings. As each element is called, each person takes their element stone to the centre with a personal blessing and thanks for that element, placing the stone on the cairn.

- ☀ Sing a chant and circle round the cairn of blessings, with your bare feet on the Earth if possible.

- ☀ Once this feels complete, pass round a length of ribbon that will encompass the whole circle without a break. When everyone is holding the ribbon, ask everyone to focus on their connection to the whole and to the Earth. How may we help? How may we radiate goodwill and generosity of Spirit in the world? How may we use the positive power of our 'yes!' to make changes for a better world? Give this a few minutes, humming together while you focus on the possibilities.

- ☀ Then pass round a pair of round-ended scissors. Let each person in turn cut themselves from the circle, holding their ribbon as they make a pledge out loud to help the Earth in some way. Then pass the scissors on to the next person. Tie the piece of ribbon to yourself as a reminder of your pledge.

☼ Holding hands again, sing and dance together, repeating the chant you began with.

☼ Close the circle by thanking each of the elements and all present.

☼ Share food, music and friendship. Dance and party! Celebrate life! Celebrate each other! Celebrate the power and beauty of the Earth!

Practise Random Kindness and Senseless Acts of Beauty

This slogan is travelling around the world, helping to change it to a more positive place for all. The idea is simply this: randomly and frequently do things that bring beauty and happiness into the world and your community. Be generous and open-hearted. Give without ulterior thought of reward, without needing recognition for your giving and without expecting thanks.

Make someone happy! Goodness goes round. Happiness is infectious. Good deeds create more good deeds. Good deeds bring happiness to giver and receiver alike. Pass this slogan on!

Vision Quest

This is a good time of year to go on a vision quest. Take a day out on your own, eat only fruit and nuts, and drink only pure spring or mineral Water. Seek inner stillness and answers to questions. Be guided by your intuition and follow your heart. Take a notebook and write down any thoughts and insights you may have. (See also page 70.)

Drying and Storing Herbs

Over the next few weeks many herbs and flowers will be ready for cutting and drying. It is best to do this just before they come into flower. Place them heads down in brown paper bags, tie them up with string and hang them to dry in a warm airy place. Label the bags clearly.

When they are completely dry, crumble them into a labelled brown paper bag or labelled dark jars. You can make your own dark herb storage jars by painting clear jam jars with dark glass paints.

Making Herb Oils

When rubbed into the skin, herb oils will be absorbed into the bloodstream and the herbs will act in the usual way. To make herb oils:

1 pint (570ml) of grapeseed oil or almond oil
3oz (85g) of fresh herb bruised between two stones
(1oz (28g) dried herb)

Place the herbs and the oil in a covered glass jar in a sunny window for one month. Shake it daily.

After a month, strain off the herbs through muslin and store the liquid in dark well-sealed bottles.

St John's Wort Oil

This is traditionally made at Midsummer. If possible, pick the plant as the flowers are just opening. Over the weeks the oil gradually turns bright red.

St John's Wort is a wonderful plant for relaxing the nervous system and its oil is a valuable anti-inflammatory and sedative, making it an excellent relaxing massage oil for tension, neuralgia, sciatica and rheumatic pains.

Drink regular infusions of the flowers (see page 35) to relieve nervous tension, irritability and anxiety, and use the infusion to bathe wounds, ulcers, shingles, herpes, bruises, rashes, varicose veins, minor burns and sunburn.

St John's Wort is uplifting to the emotions, clearing fears and phobias and bringing peaceful sleep.

Lavender Oil

Use Lavender flowers and leaves and make in the same way.

Lavender oil will ease the aches and pains of rheumatism and general weakness in the limbs. It is good for the skin, especially rough skin, sunburn and insect bites. It cleanses the bloodstream of toxins and strengthens the liver by clearing stagnation.

Use for nervous debility, exhaustion, insomnia, migraines and headaches. Lavender brings relaxation, deeper states of meditation and a general feeling of well-being and Oneness with all things.

Mapping your Locality

With the advent of good weather and light nights, this is a good time to get out and explore your locality. Create your own map of the area with your own codes, symbols and style of drawing. It doesn't have to be to scale. Mapping your locality helps you to become more observant. Try to notice things which you might otherwise pass by.

On your map, mark and name any springs, wells, streams, rivers and canals, any ancient sites, old churches, standing stones, tumuli, hills, green lanes and any special places that are important to you. Give them poetic and descriptive names that conjure up their special atmosphere.

Mark and name the trees you can identify and make a point of finding the names of those you don't know. Identification is easiest at this time of year when everything is in full leaf. Make a note of wild flowers and plants, especially edible and medicinal plants that you may need to know the location of. Watch for the spread or decline of these plants. Name and mark the location of any birds or animals that you see and any nests or burrows you notice.

As well as your map, take seasonal photos and make drawings of the trees and the views. Collect any special stories or events relating to the area, both your own adventures there and any that have been handed down through folklore and history.

If you live in a town or city, connect to its ancient past through the contours of the land, place names, old maps and very old trees such as Oak, Hawthorn and Yew. Look for the backwaters of old canals, disused railway tracks and green lanes, and find the places Nature is reclaiming.

This helps you to become connected to the land and place in which you live, is a wonderful project to do with children and provides a lasting seasonal record to look back on and add to.

Oak

Quercus robur

'Tree of courage and the doorway to inner strength'

The English Oak is an imposing tree that grows to a great size. It has large gnarled and crooked branches and a broad trunk that grows to a great girth. Many of the oldest Oaks are so wide that it takes several people holding hands to encompass them. The English countryside was once covered in Oak forests and the Oak was once a symbol of England and the strength and courage of the English people.

Oak is the 7th tree of the Celtic Tree Ogham, representing courage, inner strength, a doorway, endurance and self-determination. It is associated with Jupiter, Thor and Zeus, all mighty gods of thunder and lightning, and with durability and longevity. Known as 'the King of the Forest' and 'the King of the Trees', it holds a special place of affection in our hearts.

A slow-growing tree, Oak can live for 1,000 years. There are still many single great Oaks growing here that are famous throughout the land.

Oakwoods and Oak trees are rich in wildlife, with over 500 species of invertebrates, insects, butterflies, bats and birds all making them their home. Oak is too slow-growing and too big for a garden tree, although it can be pollarded, cut back to the crown, to keep it small. It is usually found growing in hedgerows and fields or in woods and forests.

Growing Oak Trees

Oak trees can be grown easily from the acorns, which fall in late September. Separate the acorns from the cups and put them in a bowl of water. Plant the ones that sink. Sow them straight into the ground in prepared seedbeds or large pots of compost. Keep them moist at all times, as they will not tolerate drying out, and protect them from mice with wire mesh. The roots grow first in the Winter and the first shoots appear the following April. When large enough, transplant the young Oaks into the wild during the Winter months. They grow best on deep fertile clays and loams.

Folklore and Legend

In the past Oaks were planted to mark boundaries, as they were so long-lived. Large single Oaks were used as meeting places for the passing of laws, for the crowning of kings and for the public reading of declarations and charters. The Druids taught under them and used them for ceremonies. Later the clergy would read the psalms and gospels under them as they walked the parish boundaries. These Oaks became known as 'Gospel Oaks'.

It was considered to be very fortunate to be married under an Oak. Special Oaks that were used for this became known as 'Marriage Oaks' and they continued to be popular long after the church had banned the practice. Newly weds would go straight from the church to carve their initials into the bark.

The sky gods were said to love the Oak and showed their affection by sending down their power through their lightning bolts, which frequently strike Oak trees. Pieces of charred wood from Oak trees that had been struck were kept as charms against lightning striking twice.

Mistletoe was also considered to be a gift from the sky gods. It was thought to fall from Heaven, creating a sacred marriage between Heaven and Earth. When it grew on the Oak it was especially sacred.

In Celtic legend Oak was associated with the Dagda, the chief of the old Irish gods, and Herne the Hunter, the wild male spirit of Nature, whose horns were said to resemble the branches of the Oak.

The Oakleaf was used as a symbol of strength and longevity and was engraved on English coins until the lion replaced it. Oakleaves and acorns are often used in heraldry, coats of arms and family crests.

The acorn is a potent symbol of immortality and the strength and power of Nature: 'Mighty Oaks from little acorns grow'. Acorns were carved onto the ends of wands and carried in the pocket along with Oakleaves to bring increased strength and vitality. Acorn-shaped bobbins were hung on window blinds and acorns were carved onto the fireplace as charms against lightning. Oak boughs were placed in windows and on chimneybreasts for the same reason.

Associated with Midsummer Solstice, the Oak represents the doorway to the second half of the year and to the strength that is found within. Great Midsummer fires, traditionally of Oak and known as 'Beacon Fires', were burnt on the hilltops.

The Wisdom of Oak

The Oak represents the positive power of Nature and inner strength. It is linked to Herne the Hunter, bringing us nearer to the Spirit of the Earth, teaching us that we can find solutions to our problems when we connect to the Earth for inner guidance.

Go and sit with the Oak when you feel weary of life's challenges. Oak helps us to let go of responsibilities, brings a renewal of energy and a reconnection to the simple pleasures of life. It warns us about stubborn strength that resists the winds of change and breaks in the storm.

The Wood and Its Uses

Oakwood is dense and hard, and the girth of the trunks would have made it a formidable task to fell an Oak even with metal tools.

The wood is practically indestructible. Oak logs have been dug up from peat bogs, having been submerged for thousands of years, and still been found to be fit for rough building purposes. Black bog Oak is so hard that it cannot be sawn by hand.

During the Middle Ages, Oak became the main construction material for houses and for shipbuilding. Many of the royal forests were planted with Oak to ensure a plentiful supply for the British naval fleets. Oaks were also felled in great numbers to provide a hot burning charcoal for the smiths' forges to work the metal for weapons and tools.

Oak bark was used extensively by the leather industry to provide tanning for the raw hides.

Oak roots were used to make handles which were considered to be not only strong but also magically potent.

Young light Oak branches are still much in demand for furniture making and for doors and coffins.

If you find an Oak branch that has recently broken from the main tree, cut yourself a healing wand or Ogham stick. Look for the five-pointed star hidden inside the smaller twigs.

Herbal and Edible Uses: *Quercus robur*

Bark

Take only small patches in April or May and dry it in brown paper bags. Drink a decoction (see page 35) to tone the mucous membranes and help catarrh and sinus congestion. It will also tone muscles throughout the circulatory system, making it a good remedy for varicose veins. It tones the pelvic and abdominal muscles and can be used to heal infections and inflammations of the bladder and inflamed glands.

Externally, use as a gargle for bleeding gums or mouth ulcers and for tonsillitis or laryngitis. It can be used as a lotion for chilblains, varicose veins, cuts and burns.

Leaves

Bruise and use directly to staunch bleeding. Apply directly to wounds and any inflammation.

Make an infusion of the leaves (see page 35) and add to a bowl of warm water to soak weary feet.

Oak is valued as an antidote to the effects of alcohol and to control alcohol craving. Drink daily to help with withdrawal symptoms.

Acorns

These contain large amounts of carbohydrates and fats and our ancestors roasted them in the embers of the fire and ground them between stones to make flour. Later they were used to fatten livestock, especially pigs.

Acorn Coffee
Roast the peeled kernels in a heavy frying pan until golden.
Grind and then roast them again.

Oak Flower Remedy

This is for those who are struggling bravely on, never complaining or showing weakness. It helps to ease this pressure, to bring relaxation and inner strength.

Healing Properties

Sit with the Oak when you need the strength and courage to carry on. It will bring deep calm and inner peace, helping you to sort out your problems from the inside.

Oak leads the way to truth, especially about layers of past actions, helping you sort out complicated problems and creating a gateway to a new understanding.

It restores the will and determination that may have become weakened by times of stress, helping to restore our faith in our own visions and path.

The homoeopathic remedy Quercus is used for the effects of alcoholism and problems relating to excess alcoholic consumption, such as liver problems, gout, enlarged spleen, nervousness, depression and craving for alcohol.

Spirit of
Oak

Lammas

'Festival of Gratitude and First Seeds'

End of July/beginning of August in the Northern Hemisphere

End of January/beginning of February in the Southern Hemisphere

Lammas is the time of the grain harvest, providing the basic food that will sustain us throughout the Winter. It is important to recognize that this grain is also the seed that becomes next year's harvest, the seed that lives on and completes the cycle.

Lammas gives us the opportunity to give thanks to the Earth for her abundance and to express our gratitude for our own personal harvest. As the energy of the Sun begins to wane, we begin to acknowledge the path within and assimilate what we have learned during the busy growth period. We begin to transform our outer achievements into the seeds of our future that we will nurture within.

In the past, after all the hard work of gathering in the grain harvest, it was time for community celebrations of all kinds. It was traditionally a time for tribal assessment and the choosing of new tribal leaders. Great Lammas fairs, trading fairs and horse fairs were held all over the countryside. It was a time for revelry, feasting, games and marriages, for travelling, trading and making the most of the good weather.

Lammas Celebrations

This is a time for community gatherings of all kinds, fairs, camps, local events and community projects. Whatever you do, do it together. Make a difference by sharing. Share music and songs, creativity and talents, entertainment and games. Bring all ages together to find the true heart of your community. Involve your neighbours, friends and family.

Decide on a place to meet for a shared picnic, on the common, by the
river or in the park. Bring drums and musical instruments to play.

🌿 Decorate a central tree or feature. Use flowers, grasses, stones and
twigs, anything from Nature that you can find nearby.

🌿 Create a Grain Mother together, using tied bundles of wheat, oats,
barley and grasses, and place her in the centre of the celebration.
Bunches of flowers and grasses and other creations can be added.

🌿 Bring something baked with flour, such as bread, biscuits and cakes,
in celebration of the grain harvest. Lay these out on colourful cloths
around the Grain Mother.

🌿 Ask everyone to bring something for a 'Basket of Abundance'. Put
something in and take something out that someone else has put in.

🌿 Bring food and drink to share, play music together, organize some
fun non-competitive games and enjoy your community!

A chant:

'Put your feet on the ground
And your head in the Air
And dance your dream awake.
Dance your dream awake.'

Lammas Ceremony

🪶 Create a beautiful central shrine outside. Use bunches of grasses tied with ribbon, sheaves of wheat and other grains and bunches of herbs, cut and ready to dry. Mark each of the elements in its own direction using a Hazel pole with appropriate-coloured ribbons tied to it.

🪶 Decorate each other by making headdresses out of grasses and flowers, daisy chains, garlands, ribbons and scarves.

🪶 Gather the group together with a lively chant, circling the central shrine and dancing as you sing.

🪶 Begin with a short grounding exercise, feeling the Earth beneath your feet and dropping your energy down through your body, down into the Earth, creating strong roots and a stable foundation. Enjoy a moment of silence and stillness to reflect on your gratitude and the abundance in your life.

🪶 Open the circle by acknowledging the Five Elements, dancing round the circle to each marker pole as you sing the chant. Express your gratitude to each element for the way it touches your life. Share this with each other and celebrate each personal statement together.

🪶 Pass round the circle a beautiful bunch of wheat, grasses and flowers, tied with a ribbon. As each person holds this, they share with the group what they are grateful for at this time. It is then placed at the centre of the circle.

🪶 Pass round a bowl of beads and lengths of gold thread. Each person takes a thread and a bead for each blessing in their lives that they name now. (More beads of blessings can be added at another time, but it is better to concentrate on a few at a time so that each one is remembered.) These blessing beads can be worn like a necklace or used as a focus for remembering your blessings, your prayers and well wishes.

🖋 Close the circle with an uplifting chant or chorus and return to each of the direction poles to thank each element and its place in our lives. Recapture the Spirit of community and exhilaration experienced at the beginning.

🖋 Bless the food with a shared blessing. Let the music and dancing begin! Feast and party!

Seed Collecting

Now is the time to collect seedheads.

Pick them on a dry day and only take what you need, putting them into labelled paper bags and letting them dry out in the sunshine.

Once they are dry, separate the seeds from the seed cases and put them into envelopes to keep for sowing in the Spring. Label them clearly with their name, where they came from and any growing details you might know about them, such as the type of soil needed, Sun or shade, how tall they grow, when they are in flower, the colours of the flowers, if they are edible and any herbal uses you have learned.

With hardy native plants, you can also sprinkle the seeds straight into the ground. Mark the spot with a ring of white pebbles or paint the name of the plant onto a marker stone.

Make a Positive Stand to Stop GMOs

As part of taking positive action in the world, this is one issue on which we must say 'NO!'. We must say it loud and clear, for there will be no turning back.

We all recognize that genetically modified organisms are a major risk to the environment, our health and our future, and this is not a simple matter that can be put right if it goes wrong, but one that will be irreversible. We are risking ourselves, our children and the generations to come, our unique wildlife and all our rich heritage of native plants.

There is no evidence that GM crops will feed the world's poor, as the biotech industries claim. The problems of food poverty are due to the unequal distribution of resources and Water, not to agricultural technology.

Far from feeding the world, developments like the 'terminator technology', which produces plants that have no fertile seed, are endangering the self-sufficiency of people in developing countries.

On the other hand, there are many good heartwarming initiatives that support small agricultural projects, cooperatives, small organic farms and small fair-trade businesses. Fair trade and fair play will end world poverty.

How can we make our voices heard? If you find a way, then share it, pass it on. Act on it now before it is too late. Network solutions and inspired activism!

Smudge Bundles

Smudge bundles are dried aromatic herbs that are compressed together and burnt before any healing, sacred or ceremonial work. The smoke from the herbs is used to cleanse a place or to clear and purify the energy around people.

Sage, Sweetgrass, Rosemary, Lavender, Thyme and the evergreen needles of the Cedar are good smudging herbs.

Grow herbs from organic seed and honour the Spirit of the plant as it grows.

As you harvest the plants thank them for their gift. Never take the whole plant. Always leave enough foliage for the plant to carry on with its natural cycle.

Sort your cuttings out into bundles and leave them overnight to go limp. The next day bind the stalks tightly together with a fine strong natural string or strong silk thread and hang them upside down in a warm airy place out of the sunlight to dry out completely. Tighten up the binding after they have dried.

How to Smudge

Light the leaf end of your bundle and once the flame has taken hold, blow it out immediately.

Continue to blow on the bundle so that the end begins to glow, keeping a large shell or pottery dish under it to catch any smouldering herbs. Use a large feather or cupped hands to waft the smoke around the area you wish to cleanse.

Before you smudge a place or person, smudge yourself first to clear your own energy. Some people also like to offer the smoke to the Four Directions and to Spirit before they begin.

Smudge a person by wafting the smoke towards them, starting at the head, travelling down the front of the body, then travelling up the back of the body to end with the head again. If there are any areas of the body that feel sluggish or in need of healing, spend extra time smudging here. Let your intuition guide you.

At the end of smudging, place the smouldering herbs safely in a fire-proof container, raised off the ground.

Keep your smudge bundle, smudging feather and bowl in a special place.

Earth Mandala

Mandalas are circular patterns which can be created on the ground out of the things you find in Nature, maybe grasses, soil, compost, twigs, seedheads, flowers, leaves, berries and stones. The centre of the mandala can be quite detailed, but the further you get from the centre, the more materials you will need. Be guided and inspired by whatever is naturally available and use the contrast of different colours and textures.

Take a photo if you want to remember it in the perfection of the moment and then leave it to die back into the Earth.

Apple

Malus sylvestris/domestica

'Tree of abundance and the Otherworld'

The Crab Apple recolonized Britain and Europe after the Ice Age and is found growing wild throughout the countryside in hedgerows and woods. The true Crab Apple (*Malus sylvestris*) has thorns, which have been bred out by the growers of the cultivated Apple (*Malus domestica*), but they both have similar properties.

Apple is the 10th tree of the Celtic Tree Ogham, representing abundance, open-hearted generosity, cleansing and gratitude. It is associated with Venus, goddess of Love.

It makes a good hedgerow tree that tolerates cutting and a good garden tree that brings blossom in the Spring and small colourful fruit which continue to hang on the trees until late Autumn and can be used for jam making.

Growing Apple Trees

All our different varieties of Apple tree are selected and grafted onto the rootstock of the Crab Apple and this is the only way to grow the domestic apple. If you wish to grow Crab Apples, then collect the fruit from the Crab Apple when they fall in the Autumn. The seeds are brown when they are ready and need to be stratified for one Winter (see Rowan, page 73). Select and sow germinating seeds in the Spring.

Folklore and Legend

In every country Apple is regarded as a sacred and magical fruit. In Celtic lore, it represented the Earth Mother and her abundance. When cut round the middle, it reveals a five-pointed star at its heart, an ancient symbol of protection and the Five Elements. The Druids revered the Apple tree as the bearer of the sacred mistletoe, which is frequently found growing in its branches.

Apples are seen as a means to immortality and paradise. To the Norsemen, the apples of perpetual youth grew in Asgard, the home of the Gods. The Greeks believed that in the fabled isles, somewhere in the western ocean, were to be found the golden apples of the Hesperides, which bestowed immortality. Apple trees are linked to Avalon, the magical Apple lands where King Arthur was taken to heal his wounds. Avalon is associated with the Celtic Otherworld a place that exists outside our time. In this Celtic paradise, the hills are clothed with Apple trees bearing both flowers and fruit together.

The Apple was used as a symbol to enter the other realms. It was known as 'the silver bough'. Visualize holding an Apple twig in your hand as you enter the Otherworld, or hold an Apple wand as you make your journey. In the Welsh poem *Avellanau* the bard Merlin has a secret magical orchard which he carries with him on all his journeys and can enter at will.

In the ballad of Thomas the Rhymer, the Queen of the Faerie realms warns against eating any of the apples or pears in her garden, for to eat the food of the Otherworld would mean not being able to return to the land of the living.

The Apple was said to be the fruit of the Tree of Knowledge used to tempt humankind to seek understanding beyond the limitations of blind acceptance and surface reality.

Apples are offered as a gift of Love and we talk of our loved ones as 'the apple of my eye'.

At the great Lammas gatherings, cider was drunk and honoured as one of the bountiful gifts of the Apple tree. It was also used for creating altered states and poured on the ground as a libation to give something back to Earth.

Wassailing, or Apple howling, was performed around Twelfth Night, just after the Midwinter Solstice. A procession, creating large amounts of noise, was led to the orchard to toast the Apple trees with last year's cider.

Apples have long been used for divination. The number of pips inside an Apple foretold the future, especially in matters of Love and prosperity. The popular Apple games at Halloween to go back to the time when Apple trees were associated with slipping out of time and gaining knowledge from the ancestors.

The Wisdom of Apple

The sheer extravagant abundance of the Apple tree in Autumn reflects the wisdom of this tree, which teaches us how to give all in the total trust that all will be replenished. When we, like the Apple, give freely and openly, our hearts are open to receiving more. Holding back is a symptom of both greed and insecurity.

The Apple's message is to trust that our true power lies in giving. By giving we are open to the flow of abundance we have in our lives and we value and celebrate all we have in this moment.

The Wood and its Uses

Apple wood is quite heavy and dense and is a beautiful pinkish orange colour. It is often spiralled and distorted, creating strange shapes which inspire carving. It is slow to dry and will often split and warp, but once dry it stays stable. It is difficult to work because of the irregular grain that can cause tearing, but it sands and polishes well.

Because of its hardness it was used for engravers' blocks, for making set squares and other drawing instruments.

It is ideal to carve as a Love gift, for a talisman and a healing wand.

It burns hot and it is worth saving every scrap for sweet-smelling outdoor fires

Herbal and Edible Uses: *Malus sylvestris/domestica*

The properties of the Crab Apple and the domestic Apple are similar. All parts may be used: fruit, peel, bark, blossom and leaves.

Bark

To use the bark, strip it from a small area of the tree, taking care not to ring around the tree or it will die. A decoction (see page 35) will bring down the temperature of a fever, tightening the tissues and constricting distended blood vessels.

Fruit

Apples have always been considered a tonic and a cure-all. They are an invaluable source of minerals and vitamins. 'An apple a day keeps the doctor away' is the old adage! Only eat organic apples and eat them raw whenever possible to get the full benefit of the goodness. They are very digestible and will help in the digestion of other foods. Eat daily to lower cholesterol levels and for rheumatism, diarrhoea, hypertension, anaemia, kidney and gastric problems.

A ripe juicy apple at bedtime will cure constipation and will promote sleep. Apple is also an excellent dentifrice; it not only cleans teeth but also is hard enough to push back gums so that the borders are clear of deposits.

Apples are a traditional herbal treatment for cleansing both internal and external wounds. They are anti-inflammatory and antiseptic. A poultice made from the boiled or roasted fruit, when cooled, will remove burn marks from the skin, as it helps heal skin tissue. The same boiled fruit is good for sore or inflamed eyes.

Pectin in the apple is a good germicide and promotes the growth of new skin tissue, providing a basis for the folk cure of rubbing warts with two halves of an apple and then burying them.

Apple juice and verjuice (*see below*) can also be used for burns, scalds and sprains. Rotten apples have been used as a poultice for rheumatism.

Verjuice
Make a heap of ripe Crab Apples and leave them until they
begin to sweat.
Remove the stalks and rotten fruit, beat the remainder to a mush
in a large bowl and then press it through muslin or a coarse cloth.
Bottle the verjuice, which will be ready to drink in one month.

Crab Apple Jelly
Crab Apples are high in pectin, which helps jam to set, and they can be added to any other fruit for this purpose.

To make Crab Apple jelly:
Rough chop 6lb (2.7kg) of fruit and boil in Water with
a slice of ginger root and a chopped lemon.
Pour the pulp into a jelly bag and let it drip overnight.
Do not squeeze!
Return the liquid to the pan and add 1lb (450g) of sugar
to each pint (0.567 litre) of juice.
Rapid boil for half an hour until the jelly shows signs of setting
when tested on a cold plate.

Crab Apple Flower Remedy

This is the remedy for cleansing. People in need of the Crab Apple remedy tend to be more than usually sensitive, sometimes having a poor self-image and becoming over-anxious about physical cleanliness and contamination or stuck in details.

The remedy can be used directly on wounds as a cleanser, especially if it is believed that there has been some poisoning. It can also be added to the bath Water to bring a renewal of Spirit.

It is recommended when fasting, to cleanse the body of toxins and also to overcome the effects of a hangover (four drops every hour).

Healing Properties

Apple helps us to get in touch with our sense of abundance. If you do not feel worthy to receive certain things then the way for them to come to you will be blocked, as you have believed it to be. By affirming and feeling thankful for what you have in the present, you open the channels for your own abundance.

Apple brings healing to the Spirit, helping us to embrace the abundant world within ourselves, expanding our ability to travel within and gain access to knowledge and understanding beyond our rational minds.

Spirit of
Apple

Autumn Equinox

'Festival of Harvest and Gratitude'

20–23 September in the Northern Hemisphere

20–23 March in the Southern Hemisphere

Now day and night are equal in both hemispheres.

We too experience balance and integration as we reconnect to our inner selves. We become aware of the changing season, which gives us the chance to start again. This is a good time to release the past and move forward with clarity as we begin to prepare for the coming Winter and to incubate new seeds within.

This is a time of ripening fruits, nuts, berries, mushrooms and seeds. Trees and plants are letting their energy fall back down into their roots. Leaves are dropping to Earth to make compost, rich in nutrition and goodness, providing the best conditions for future new growth.

This is the time for long-term planning and nurturing. The seeds of ideas and the seeds of hope that we plant now will re-emerge in the Spring, strengthened and consolidated by their time in the dark and stabilized by their strong roots.

It is time to celebrate the power of balance, to move beyond our old habits of polarity, the 'us and them' mentality which has led to war, misery and poverty. Now we seek inspiring new ways to bring harmony and equality into our lives and the world.

Traditionally, this is the big harvest party of Summer's end, a time to celebrate our achievements and give thanks for the Earth's abundance. The active Earth dragon withdraws and takes the Fire into the dark inner realms, providing strength, courage and wisdom from within.

Autumn Equinox Celebration

∞ Gather with friends and family to celebrate and give thanks for the abundance of the harvest and honour the completion of the growing season. Bring fruit, seasonal food and drinks to share. This is an opportunity to experience the power of generosity. Ask everyone to bring anything that they have in abundance that they wish to give away. It may be produce, plants, seeds or the fruits of their creativity or hard work.

∞ Create a beautiful harvest shrine out of the things everyone brings. Share these out at the end or give them to others who would appreciate them.

∞ Ask everyone to bring something that represents their personal harvest and display these around the harvest shrine. Don't be afraid to celebrate and share your achievements and personal harvests with each other. Be proud of what you have achieved! This helps others to be able to do the same.

∞ Give thanks for the abundance of food, friendship and community. Our gratitude opens our hearts and helps the positive flow of Love and joy to shine in our lives.

A chant:

'I find my joy in the simple things
that come from the Earth.
I find my joy in the Sun that shines
and the river that sings to me.
So listen to the wind
And listen to the Water

And hear what they say,

Singing, "Hey anana, Hey anana, Hey anana, Hey."

Let me never forget,

Never forget, to give thanks.

Give thanks, give thanks, give thanks and praise.'

Autumn Equinox Ceremony

∞ Playing drums and percussion and singing a chant, gather together in a circle of community around the central harvest shrine. Light some nightlights in bowls of sand around it and enjoy the sight of your own abundance.

∞ Open the circle by thanking and acknowledging the Five Elements and the part each one has played in creating the harvest.

∞ Pass a crystal around the circle and as each person holds it they share with everyone their personal harvest. Begin with 'I am grateful for…' and end with a reflection on the seeds inherent in this. Keep circling until everyone feels complete and place the crystal at the centre when everyone has finished.

∞ Ask everyone to contemplate what they could give back to the Earth. Pass round a bowl of Spring bulbs. Each person chooses a bulb and shares with the group what they have decided to do for the Earth. Later, as this special bulb is planted, at home or in the wild, reinforce the pledge you made today.

∞ End on a cone of power, as each person lets out whatever sounds, notes or words they wish to make, sending out their Love and commitment to the Earth and themselves. Begin with a whisper and gradually build up the sound until it reaches a peak of connection and energy, then gradually let it die back again to a whisper.

∞ Close the circle by thanking the elements and each other. Sing the chant again. Share a blessing for the food and drink, then feast and party!

Tree Planting and Growing

Now is the time for collecting and stratifying tree seeds (see Rowan, page 73) and taking cuttings to make new trees (see Elder, page 46). It is also the time for preparing the ground for tree planting.

Make sure that there is enough space for the tree to grow to maturity unless you intend to coppice it, train it against a wall or create a bower or archway.

Choose well-drained sites and prepare the ground by digging well and removing roots, weeds and large stones. Ideally, for each tree, dig an area roughly 3 feet (1 metre) wide and add some compost to enrich and lighten the soil. If there are rabbits, squirrels, deer or livestock nearby, buy biodegradable tree guards. These come in different sizes and fit around the stems of young trees to protect them from being eaten.

Trees are ready to plant after the leaves have fallen. Dig the hole big enough for the roots to spread and add more compost at the bottom of the hole. It is important that the root collar, the point from which the roots grow, is at the surface. Firm the soil around the tree with your boot and cover with a mulch such as bark chippings or a mulch mat to stop weeds. Any tree bigger than 6.5 feet (2 metres) should be staked using a stout pole driven well into the ground. Make sure the straps are not too tight and that they do not chafe the tree.

Young trees need to be looked after and you need to check them from time to time. This builds up your relationship with them. Make sure they are watered in dry weather and check the tree guards and the straps. Ideally, the

3 foot (1 metre) circle around your tree needs to be kept weed free for five years, but you can plant Spring bulbs around the base of the tree.

Grow more trees and plant more trees! Every tree we plant is helping to improve the Air around us and helping the Earth recover from the damage caused by fossil fuels from our vehicles and air travel and the legacy of the Industrial Age.

Plant a tree to commemorate a special event or a special person, a birth or a death. This then becomes their personal tree. Find land that can be used for tree planting, such as schools, parks and industrial wasteland, and encourage your community to dedicate and plant more trees!

Tree planting is also a way to offset your own personal contribution to carbon dioxide pollution and global warming (see Appendix on page 279). However, we do need to lessen our addiction to fossil fuel travel and support solar, wind, Water and hydrogen initiatives whenever we can. This also means supporting and eating locally produced food and buying locally produced goods whenever possible.

Clearing Out the Old

In our gardens at this time, we prune and cut back, clearing away all the old growth that has finished, so the plants can consolidate their strength for the Winter. This also encourages new growth in the Spring.

In our lives, too, it is a good time to make decisions about what we want to give priority to, what to cut back and what to strengthen. Clear out what is no longer helping you – outworn modes of behaviour, old patterns and habits that are holding you back and the physical things associated with them. Clearly and with gratitude, make a statement of intent to cut these things out of your life. Visualize cutting yourself free of them. Focus on the new shoots that will grow from these actions.

Making a Walking Stick

The Autumn and Winter months are the best time for cutting a walking stick, when the sap is going down and the tree is conserving its energy.

1. Look for a straight stick among the hedgerows. The weight and thickness of the stem are a matter of personal choice. The most likely trees to have straight stems are Hazel, coppiced Willow and Ash, Holly and Blackthorn (be very careful of the thorns).

2. Sit with the tree for a while and explain your wish before you cut your chosen stick with gratitude. Let the stick rest by the tree for a while. Then take it home and leave it outside for a few weeks.

3. Before you cut the stick to size, decide on the kind of handle the stick lends itself to. Let your stick guide you by its shape, features and energy. The placing of the handle is crucial to your comfort as you walk with the stick, so spend time on getting this right. Handles can be carved, but bear in mind your comfort when holding it.

4. Cut off any twigs and smooth the wood down with sandpaper (see also Hazel, page 104). If you decide to strip off the bark, it comes off more easily when the stick is first cut. After you have stripped

it, let the wood dry out and then use a rough sandpaper, then medium, then smooth for a silky finish.

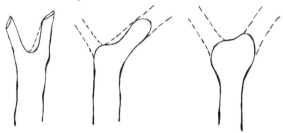

5. It is good to feed the wood to stop it becoming dry and brittle, so rub in several coats of teak oil or any similar light oil that will not change the colour of the wood and finish with several layers of beeswax polish, which can be polished up to a good shine but still allows the wood to breathe.

6. Before oiling and waxing, you can paint a design or symbol on your stick with acrylic paint or experiment with staining the wood with plant dyes. Crystals, copper wire and other natural materials may be inlaid and set into your stick using epoxy resin.

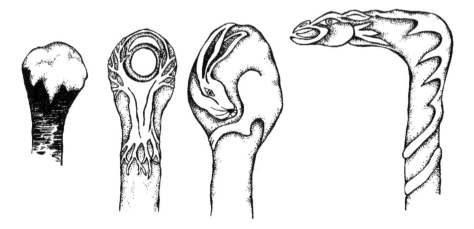

Blackthorn

Prunus spinosa

'Tree of hope and challenge'

This small tree can be found in hedgerows and woods and if left, will grow into a dense impenetrable thicket that creates a powerful barrier to human intrusion. It has long sharp thorns and any scratches should be treated with a strong antiseptic or they can become badly infected.

Blackthorn is the 14th tree of the Celtic Tree Ogham and represents a challenge and choice of perspective. It is associated with Saturn and Mars.

Blackthorn flowers are out in early March when it is often still cold. Their whiteness stands out against the black bark and otherwise bare hedgerows and is a symbol of the coming Spring.

In the Autumn the blue-black fruit, called sloes, are a symbol of the coming Winter. They are thought to be related to the damson and other domestic plums.

Blackthorn is a good hedging plant and small birds like to build their nests amongst its branches. It regenerates quickly after cutting or fire, producing suckers from below ground level.

Growing Blackthorn Trees

To grow Blackthorn, collect the sloes after the leaves have fallen. Remove the seeds from the flesh, wash thoroughly and stratify (*see Rowan, page 73*). They usually germinate the first Winter.

Folklore and Legend

A cold Spring was traditionally called a Blackthorn Winter, as little else would be out but the Blackthorn flowers.

Blackthorn itself has generally been thought of as a tree of bad luck or bad magic. The 'black rod' or 'blasting rod' was a Blackthorn stick thought to have black powers used by evil witches and magicians. The thorns can certainly do harm, causing septicaemia if the wounds are left untreated.

These superstitions have given Blackthorn a bad reputation. It was known as the keeper of dark secrets and was feared above all other trees.

Blackthorn was in fact used by the healers of the past because of its positive power of cleansing, its ability to bring increased clarity and its strong life energy. It is linked to the rune Thorn, which brings protection and good luck. The dense Blackthorn thickets kept the Romans out of Anglesey in North Wales, making it the last Druid stronghold.

The Wisdom of Blackthorn

Blackthorn has a misunderstood energy that teaches us to look beyond the surface and balance this with our intuition and a positive outlook. Everything that happens, even if it may look negative, can have a positive outcome and lead to a fruitful change. There is always another way of looking at things.

The thorns can be seen to represent our negative attitudes — sharp and dangerous to our own Spirit and to those around us.

Blackthorn thickets create good psychic barriers and teach us to be aware of when we must protect ourselves from the malicious words or actions of others.

Blackthorn teaches us that at every moment in every situation we all have a choice. One choice is positive, supporting life and Love, the other negative and destructive. We all have the choice which path we take and which world we choose to live in.

The Wood and Its Uses

The wood has light yellow sapwood and brown heartwood and is hard and tough. Both the wood and the black bark sand and polish up well to a beautiful rich shine. Traditionally, it is used for walking sticks, fighting sticks and for the Irish shillelagh or cudgel.

Herbal and Edible Uses: *Prunus spinosa*

Flowers

Make an infusion of the flowers (see page 35) for the treatment of fevers, blood disorders, lack of appetite, worms, bladder problems, skin problems and stomach cramps. This is a gentle laxative and has a beneficial effect on the stomach. Eat a handful of the flowers every morning as a general early Spring tonic.

Leaves

An infusion of the leaves (see page 35) makes an excellent mouthwash and gargle for tonsillitis and laryngitis and once cool, can be used as a soothing eyebath.

Bark

Make a decoction of the bark (see page 35) as a sedative and a calming tea for all nervous disorders. Collect only small pieces and shave them finely.

Fruit

The sloes are best picked after the first frosts have softened them. They can also be rendered sweeter by burying them in straw-lined pits deep in the ground for several months.

Add to other hedgerow fruit to make hedgerow jam and also use for making wine. The juice makes a natural red dye and was used as marking ink.

Sloe Gin

1. Fill one third of a wide-necked jar with pricked sloes.
2. Make it up to half full with sugar and then fill to the top with gin or vodka.
3. Shake daily for three months and watch the gin turn deep red.

4. Strain off the fruit, but do not squeeze.

5. Rebottle, keeping some for the Solstice and some to save for one year for an improved flavour.

6. Rather than throw the gin-soaked fruit away, cut the flesh from the stones and add to melted chocolate or chocolate cake!

Healing Properties

Blackthorn helps us to remember that there is always a choice in the direction of our thoughts, our actions and our spirituality. Instead of war we can choose cooperation. Instead of struggle we can choose balance and union. Instead of revenge we can choose to share our feelings and develop understanding. Instead of 'us and them' we can choose 'We'.

We can learn to trust in our own integrity and find loving solutions to our problems to bring a fruitful outcome. We can choose to walk towards our most positive visions and hold them strong in our minds and hearts without giving up. True spirituality is found through the power of Love, bringing any difficult situation to a positive conclusion.

Blackthorn has the ability to move deep blockages, bringing cleansing and release and a new direction. Out of a difficult or negative situation can come an opportunity for positive action. This is its gift.

Spirit of Blackthorn

Endpiece

This cycle of course doesn't end here; it is just another new beginning. Each festival is experienced in relation to the one that went before and the one that comes next. We are evolving and growing with every end and every new beginning.

Each cycle helps us to become more aware of our beautiful Earth and our unfolding understanding of ourselves.

Each cycle creates new opportunities to follow our path of the heart. By being guided by our gratitude, our Love, our goodwill and our generosity, all our actions form part of a growing connected family of people bringing positive change into the world.

We are living in extraordinary times and I am open to the exciting possibility that a miracle is about to happen as we experience a collective shift in consciousness that is creating a more caring and loving world in which we are growing.

WE are the change and together we are making a difference!

Appendix

Exhortation: Towards a True Balance

Available as an A4 poster, greetings cards and reuse envelope labels.
Send stamped addressed envelope for details to: 'SECRET GARDENS',
Manor Farm Cottage, Rendham, Saxmundham, Suffolk IP17 2AH, UK

Offsetting your Personal CO_2 Pollution

Car Commuting

Highly efficient car (36–56 mpg):
Up to 5,000 miles: Plant 3 trees.
5,000–10,000 miles: Plant 6 trees.

Efficient car (26–36 mpg):
Up to 5,000 miles: Plant 4 trees.
5,000–10,000 miles: Plant 8 trees.

4x4, van, large car:
Up to 5,000 miles: Plant 9 trees.
5,000–10,000 miles: Plant 16 trees.

Flying

One return flight from the UK:

To Europe: Plant 2 trees.
To USA (East Coast): Plant 4 trees.
To USA (West Coast): Plant 6 trees.
India: Plant 6 trees.
Thailand: Plant 9 trees.
South Africa: Plant 9 trees.
Australia: Plant 10 trees.
New Zealand: Plant 16 trees.

Many of the tree organizations listed in Networking Solutions will plant trees on your behalf.

References
and
Inspirational Reading

Creativity

Diana Carey and Judy Large, *Festivals, Family and Food*, Hawthorn Press, 1982

Stephanie Cooper, Christine Fynes-Clinton and Marye Rowling, *The Children's Year*, Hawthorn Press, 1986

Gordon MacLellan, *Talking to the Earth*, Capall Bann Publishing, 1996

Earth Energies

Robin Heath, *Sun, Moon and Earth*, Wooden Books, 1999

John Martineau, *Mazes and Labyrinths in Great Britain*, Wooden Books, 2000

Don Robins, *Circles of Silence, The Dragon Project*, Souvenir Press, 1985

Serena Roney-Dougal, *The Faery Faith: An Integration of Science with Spirit*, Green Magic Publishing, 2002

T. Edward Ross and Richard D. Wright, *The Divining Mind: A Guide to Dowsing and Self-Awareness*, Destiny Books, 1990

Healing/Self-Help

Edward Bach, *Heal Thyself*, C. W. Daniel, 1996; first published 1931

Denise Linn, *Sacred Space*, Rider Press, 1996

Ervin Laszlo, *You Can Change the World*, Positive News Publishing Ltd, 2002

Louise Hay, *You Can Heal Your Life*, Hay House, Inc., 1984

Peter Aziz, *Spirit Allies from the Plant Kingdom*, Points Press, 1997

Elizabeth Brooke, *A Woman's Book of Herbs*, The Women's Press, 1992

Mrs M. Grieves, *A Modern Herbal*, Tiger Books International, 1994; first published 1931

Judith Hoad, *Healing with Herbs*, Gill and Macmillan, 1996

Anne McIntyre, *The Complete Floral Healer*, Gaia Books, 1996

The Natural World

Anand Chetan and Diana Brueton, *The Sacred Yew: Rediscovering the Ancient Tree of Life through the Work of Allen Meredith*, Arkana, 1994

Elizabeth Edwards, Finnuala O'Hare, Kath Simmonds, Jill Taylor and Sue Weaver, *Sanctuary: Finding a New Relationship with the Land*, Permanent Publications, 2002

John Martineau, *The Little Book of Coincidence*, Wooden Books, 2001

Jacqueline Memory Paterson, *Tree Wisdom: The Definitive Guidebook to the Myth, Folklore and Healing Power of Trees*, Thorsons, 1996

Inspirational Magazines
and
Publications

Ethical Consumer

Promoting change and empowering the consumer. Helping you to become proactive and make an informed choice about what you buy. All the latest news, buyer's guides, research, in-depth reports and boycotts.

ECRA Publishing Ltd, Unit 21, Old Birley Street, Manchester, M15 5RF, UK

Tel: 0161 226 2929

E-mail: mail@ethicalconsumer.org

www.ethicalconsumer.org

Ode

An international news magazine with a passion for people. Inspiring articles by leading thinkers and pioneers of progress. Exploring new opportunities and visions to make the world a better place, Ode combines positive ideas with practical solutions.

Ode Magazine, PO Box 2402, 3000 CK Rotterdam, The Netherlands

Tel: +31 10 4360 995

E-mail: ode@odemagazine.com

www.odemagazine.com

Permaculture Magazine: Solutions for Sustainable Living

Thought-provoking, practical, positive and open-minded solutions for creating a more sustainable lifestyle.

Permanent Publications, Hyden House Ltd, The Sustainability Centre, East Meon, Hampshire, GU32 1HR, UK

Tel: 0845 458 4150

E-mail: enquiries@permaculture.co.uk

www.permaculture.co.uk

Positive News

A quarterly newspaper and magazine of positive news from around the world.

Positive News, No. 5 Bicton Enterprise Centre, Clun, Shropshire, SY7 8NF, UK

Tel: 01588 640 022

E-mail: office@positivenews.org.uk

Small World

Practical answers to poverty.

ITDG, The Schumacher Centre for Technology and Development, Bourton Hall, Bourton-on-Dunsmore, Rugby, CV23 9QZ, UK

Tel: 01926 634 400

Networking Solutions

The British Association of Dowsers

2 St Ann's Road, Malvern, Worcestershire, WR14 4RG, UK

Tel: 01684 576 969

www.britishdowsers.org

Environmental Transport Association

Supporting and campaigning for a sustainable transport system. Includes a breakdown service and informative magazine.

Tel: 0800 212 810

www.eta.co.uk

Friends of the Earth

Inspires solutions to environmental problems.

26–28 Underwood Street, London N1 7JQ, UK

Tel: 020 7490 1555

www.foe.co.uk

Friends of the Trees

Creating special places of contemplation, peace and mutual friendship in nature. Promoting sacred groves in the British Isles and protecting ancient trees, particularly Yews.

Friends of the Trees, The Secretary, 31 Bisley Rd, Stroud, GL5 1HF, UK

E-mail: info@FriendsOfTheTrees.org.uk

www.FriendsOfTheTrees.org.uk

Greenpeace

Non-violent, creative confrontation to expose global environmental problems and their causes.
Canonbury Villas, London N1 2PN, UK
Tel: 020 7490 1555
www.greenpeace.org.uk

The Permaculture Association

Using the ethics and principles of permaculture and playing an active part in the developing culture of positive change.
BCM Permaculture Association, London WC1N 3XX, UK
Tel: 0845 458 1805
www.permaculture.org.uk

Shared Interest

Investing in fair trade. Strengthening the fair trade movement.
Tel: 0845 840 9100
www.shared-interest.com

The Small Woods Association

Bringing together all those with an interest in small woods. Help with woodland ownership, events, training courses, magazine.
The Small Woods Association, The Old Bakery, Pontesbury, Shropshire, ST5 5RR, UK
E-mail: enquiries@smallwoods.org.uk
www.smallwoods.org.uk

The Soil Association

Campaigning for organic food and farming and sustainable forestry.

Bristol House, 40–56 Victoria Street, Bristol, BS1 6BY, UK

Tel: 0117 929 0661

www.soilassociation.org

The Tree Council

Making trees matter to everyone. Projects, planting programmes, events, campaigns and Tree News, an informative magazine linking major tree organizations in the UK.

E-mail: enquiries@treenews.org.uk

www.treecouncil.org.uk

Tree Spirit

A registered charity and voluntary active group planting and growing trees for our future, combining practical conservation with a holistic approach raising awareness and respect for trees. Membership includes lively magazine and practical work camps on Tree Spirit land.

Membership enquiries to: Emma and Liam Dowling, 84 Stepping Stones Road, Coundon, Coventry, CV5 8JU, UK

General correspondence to: Tree Spirit, Hawkbatch Farm, Arley, Nr Bewdley, Worcestershire, DY12 3AH. Please include a stamped addressed envelope for your reply.

Trees for Life

A Scottish conservation charity dedicated to the regeneration and restoration of the Caledonian forest in the highlands of Scotland. Tree planting programmes, volunteer work and projects.
The Park, Findhorn Bay, Forres, IV36 3TZ, Scotland
Tel: 0845 4583505
E-mail: trees@findhorn.org
www.treesforlife.org.uk

Triodos Bank

Ethical banking. Triodos only lends money to organizations and businesses pursuing positive social, environmental and cultural goals.
Brunel House, 11 The Promenade, Bristol, BS8 3NN, UK
Tel: 0117 973 9339
www.triodos.co.uk

Turning the Tide

Promoting the understanding and use of active non-violence as an effective way of bringing about change.
Friends House, 173 Euston Rd, London, NW1 2BJ, UK
Tel: 020 7663 1064/ 1061
www.turning-the-tide.org

The Woodland Trust

Protecting our native heritage. Campaigns, events, tree planting, magazine.
Tel: 01476 581 136
www.woodland-trust.org.uk

Additional Websites

Centre for Implosion Research (Bringing water back to life):
www.implosionresearch.com

Earth Charter: www.earthcharter.org

Ethical Investment Research Service: www.eiris.org

International Forum on Globalization: www.ifg.org

Transnational Institute (promotes international cooperation solutions):
www.tni.org

Index

Repertory

Herbal remedies in this book

A

abdominal muscles 238
alcohol addiction 239
anaemia 256
anti inflammatory 231, 256
antiseptic 17, 77
appetite, lack 273
arteries, hardening 220

B

bladder problems 17, 238, 273
blood cleanser 231
blood disorders 273
blood pressure (high) 220
broken bones 169
bruises 49, 231
burns 49, 201, 231, 238, 257

C

catarrh 49, 168, 238
chilblains 238
cholesterol, lowers 256
circulation 220, 238
cleanser 17, 256
colds 50, 168
congestion 50, 238
constipation 256
coughs 50, 168
cuts 49, 238
cystitis 17

D

diarrhoea 256

About the Author

I live in Derbyshire, England, with my partner, musician and songwriter Brian Boothby, and our two teenagers. As well as writing and illustrating books, I am an artist, an art, pottery and crafts teacher, an events coordinator, a celebrant and a creator of meditation gardens and labyrinths.

I am available for commissions involving any of the above.

I enjoy giving workshops and encourage an uplifting and creative experience. My workshops can be adapted according to the needs of your group.

The Sacred Tree Workshop

This is a experience of native British trees and can include a talk, tree meditations, tree journeys, the Celtic Tree Ogham, working with the energy of trees, communicating with Dryads, tree ceremonies, tree walks, tree identification, making walking sticks, talismans, healing wands, pendants, touchwoods and Ogham sticks. Elementary woodworking skills are taught and tools are provided.

Hearthfire

This is a daylong workshop that tunes into the developing energy of the Earth and ourselves at each of the Celtic festivals. It includes meditation, inner journeying, ceremony, drumming, chanting and sharing to bring clarity, renewal and new directions. These insights and connections form the basis for creating a sacred art piece or artefact to take home at the end of the day. No art skills are needed and all materials are provided.

You are encouraged to find your own sacred connections, express your own personal creativity and become aware of the potential of your own wisdom.

If you wish to write to me, Hay House UK will be pleased to forward your letters. Please include a stamped addressed envelope for your reply.

Please write to:

Hay House UK, Ltd, Unit 62, Canalot Studios, 222 Kensal Rd, London W10 5BN, UK

Other Books by Glennie Kindred

Earth Cycles of Celebration, Glennie Kindred, 1991, revised 2002

Sacred Tree, Glennie Kindred, 1995, revised 2003

The Tree Ogham, Glennie Kindred, 1997

Herbal Healers, Wooden Books, 1999, revised 2002

Hedgerow Cookbook, Wooden Books, 1999, revised 2002

Sacred Celebrations, Gothic Image, 2001

Creating Ceremony, with Lu Garner, Glennie Kindred, 2002

All publications and many of the illustrations are available from
the author. Please send a stamped addressed envelope
to Hay House Publishers for a catalogue.

We hope you enjoyed this Hay House book.
If you would like to receive a free catalogue featuring additional
Hay House books and products or if you would like information about
the Hay Foundation, please contact:

Hay House UK, Ltd

Unit 62, Canalot Studios

222 Kensal Road, London W10 5BN

Phone: 44 20 8962 1230 or Fax: 44 20 8962 1239

www.hayhouse.co.uk

***

Distributed in the United States by:
Hay House, Inc., P.O. Box 5100, Carlsbad, CA 92018-5100
Phone: 760-431-7695 or 800-654-5126
Fax: 760-431-6948 or 800-650-5115
www.hayhouse.com

Distributed in Australia by:
Hay House Australia Pty Ltd.
18/36 Ralph St., Alexandria NSW 2015
Phone: 61-2-9669-4299
Fax: 61-2-9669-4144
www.hayhouse.com.au

Distributed in Canada by:
Raincoast, 9050 Shaughnessy St., Vancouver, B.C. V6P 6E5
Phone: 604-323-7100
Fax: 604-323-2600

Distributed in the Republic of South Africa by:
Hay House SA (Pty), Ltd., P.O. Box 990, Witkoppen 2068
Phone/Fax: 27-11-701-2233
orders@psdprom.co.za